Teach Yourself®

Beginners'
Mandarin Chinese

Elizabeth Scurfield and Song Lianyi

First published in UK as *Get Started in Mandarin Chinese* by Hodder & Stoughton in 1996

This edition published by Teach Yourself in 2024

An imprint of John Murray Press

1

Copyright © Elizabeth Scurfield and Song Lianyi 1996, 2003, 2010, 2013, 2024

The right of Elizabeth Scurfield and Song Lianyi to be identified as the Author of the Work has been asserted by them in accordance with the Copyright, Designs and Patents Act 1988.

Illustrations by Nadene Naude (Beehive Illustration)

Editorial support from Haremi Ltd

All rights reserved. No part of this publication may be reproduced, stored in a retrieval system, or transmitted, in any form or by any means without the prior written permission of the publisher, nor be otherwise circulated in any form of binding or cover other than that in which it is published and without a similar condition being imposed on the subsequent purchaser.

A CIP catalogue record for this title is available from the British Library

Paperback ISBN 9781399818223
ebook ISBN 9781399819374

Typeset by Integra Software Services Pvt. Ltd., Pondicherry, India

Printed and bound in Great Britain by Clays Ltd, Elcograf S.p.A.

John Murray Press policy is to use papers that are natural, renewable and recyclable products and made from wood grown in sustainable forests. The logging and manufacturing processes are expected to conform to the environmental regulations of the country of origin.

John Murray Press	Nicholas Brealey Publishing
Carmelite House	Hachette Book Group
50 Victoria Embankment	Market Place, Center 53, State Street
London EC4Y 0DZ	Boston, MA 02109, USA

www.teachyourself.com

John Murray Press, part of Hodder & Stoughton Limited

An Hachette UK company

Contents

	Meet the authors	vi
	How the book works	vii
	Learn to learn	xiii
	The Mandarin language	xvii
	Abbreviations	xx
	Pronunciation guide	xxi
	Useful expressions	xxvii
	The written language	xxx
1	**Nǐ hǎo! Nǐ hǎo ma?** *Hello! How are you?*	2
	Saying hello and goodbye • Exchanging greetings • Saying please and thank you • Making a simple apology • Observing basic courtesies	
2	**Nǐ jiào shénme?** *What's your name?*	14
	Saying who you are • Making simple introductions • Asking who other people are • Addressing people correctly • Denying something	
3	**Nǐ shì nǎ guó rén?** *Where are you from?*	26
	Saying where you come from and what nationality you are • Asking for and giving an address • Numbers 0–10 • Asking for and giving a phone number • Filling out a form	
4	**Nǐ yǒu xiōngdì jiěmèi ma?** *Do you have brothers and sisters?*	40
	Talking about yourself and your family • Asking other people about their family • Asking someone if they are married and/or have children • Saying how old you are • Asking how old somebody is • Counting up to 100	

5 Jǐ diǎn le? *What time is it now?* — 54
Days of the week • Months of the year • Telling the time • Asking what time it is • Useful expressions of time • Giving the date • Making arrangements

Review 1 — 68

6 Nǐ jīntiān xiǎng zuò shénme? *What do you want to do today?* — 70
Saying what you want to do • Understanding and asking for advice • Expressing similarities • Comparing and contrasting

7 Duōshao qián? *How much is it?* — 84
Asking for things (in shops) • Asking the price • Stating quantities • Numbers 100–1000 • Expressing the distance between two points

8 Zěnmeyàng? *What's it like?* — 102
Asking about sizes • Talking about clothes and shoes • Describing things • Expressing likes and dislikes • Making comparisons

9 Qù . . . zěnme zǒu? *How do I get to . . . ?* — 116
Asking for and understanding directions • Using public transport • Asking people if they have ever done something • Expressing how long something happens for

10 Nín xiǎng chī shénme? *What would you like to eat?* — 132
Ordering a meal and drinks • Paying the bill • Saying you have given up something • More about verb endings

Review 2 — 146

Answer key — 149

Chinese–English vocabulary — 168

English–Chinese vocabulary — 174

Appendix: character texts — 181

Can-do statements — 198

Dedications

In memory of a much loved mother, Ella Jessie Scurfield, whose loving spirit and quiet courage will always be with me.

To Rong, my wife, whose support has been invaluable.

Meet the authors

Elizabeth Scurfield and Song Lianyi are both experienced and enthusiastic teachers of Chinese. Elizabeth Scurfield graduated with a first-class honours degree in Chinese from the School of Oriental and African Studies in London and has taught Chinese for over 40 years, 30 of them at university level. She was co-founder of the Chinese Department at the University of Westminster (1974) at the age of 23 and brought new ideas and enthusiasm to its creation. She has made numerous short and extended visits and study trips to China since her first visit in 1976 as the only woman participant on a delegation of younger sinologists.

Song Lianyi (Song being the surname) grew up in China. He obtained his BA in China and his MA and PhD in the UK. Currently he is Principal Teaching Fellow in Chinese at the School of Oriental and African Studies, University of London, where he has taught Chinese for over 30 years. He has been an active member of the British Chinese Language Teaching Society and is a life member of the International Society for Chinese Language Teaching.

Elizabeth Scurfield and Song Lianyi were colleagues in the same university nearly 30 years ago and their fruitful collaboration has continued ever since. In addition to *Beginners' Mandarin Chinese*, their current titles in the Teach Yourself series include *Get Talking Mandarin Chinese in Ten Days*, *Keep Talking Mandarin Chinese* and *Read and Write Chinese Script*.

Elizabeth Scurfield and Song Lianyi

How the book works

WHY CHINESE?

Written documentation on the development of Chinese goes back nearly four thousand years, making Chinese the oldest language on the planet. And, as the speakers of the language have developed and changed over this time, so too has the language itself. Probably the main change would be the apparent simplification of the form of the language, resulting in the 'alphabet' (i.e. character set) consisting of a mere 400 or so syllables. And yet the language continues to be vibrant and evolving, due to the extensions possible through compounding and tonal additions.

WHICH CHINESE WILL YOU BE LEARNING?

In one form or another, Chinese is the language most spoken in the world. It has many different spoken forms, but they are all written in almost exactly the same way, the difference being that the simplified script is used in the People's Republic of China and in Singapore and that full-form characters are used in Taiwan and Hong Kong. The characters used in this book are always in the simplified script. For more information on the Chinese script, you can refer to *Read and Write Chinese Script* and to *Complete Chinese*.

More than 70% of Chinese people speak the northern dialect so the national language is based on this. More Chinese speakers can understand this national language than any other form of Chinese so it is what you will be learning in this book. In China it is called **pǔtōnghuà** (*common speech*), but it is sometimes referred to in the West as Modern Standard Chinese.

WHAT IS ROMANIZATION?

Chinese cannot be written using a phonetic alphabet in the way that European languages can. It is written in characters. You will find out more about characters in the section on the written language. Various ways have been devised for representing Chinese sounds alphabetically. The standard form in use today is known as **pīnyīn** (literally *spell sound*) and is what we have used in this book. In 1958 **pīnyīn** was adopted as the official system of romanization in the People's Republic of China. Please note that **pīnyīn** is not an accurate phonetic transliteration of Chinese sounds for English speakers.

Now welcome to *Beginners' Mandarin Chinese*, a course designed for complete beginners! It is a self-study course that will help you to understand and speak Chinese sufficiently well to function effectively in basic everyday situations, both business and social. The course will also offer you an insight into Chinese culture and there is even an opportunity for you to find out something about the Chinese writing system if you want to.

Chinese is a fascinating language to study and quite unique, with a completely different alphabet, a grammar structure entirely different to English and sounds unlike any of those of the common European languages. Learning Chinese may seem difficult at first but you mustn't be put off. Keep going and you will quickly begin to spot the patterns and understand how things work.

How to use this book

A little goes a long way!

Try to use the book little and often, rather than for long stretches at a time (between 15 and 30 minutes if possible, rather than two to three hours in one session). This will help you to create a study habit, much in the same way you would practice a sport or music. Leave the book somewhere handy so that you can pick it up for just a few minutes to refresh your memory again with what you were looking at the time before.

Before you start, make a plan!

Setting goals affects the programming of your brain, strengthening neural pathways and ultimately making it more likely that you will achieve those goals. Before you begin, think about how much time you want to devote to learning, which skills or areas you want to focus on, and identify specific ideas you want to be able to communicate or activities you want to engage in.

Track your progress!

Start a notebook to use for study, where you can create vocabulary lists, a grammar summary, questions you'd like answered, etc. Keep track of your resources – write down the names of films, podcasts, songs or blogs you like, and jot down a few words or expressions you may have recognized or learned. The more you can reflect on your learning process, the deeper your connection with the language will be. If you need more guidance in this process, we recommend Teach Yourself *Fluentish: Language Learning Planner & Journal* by Jo Franco.

Use the tools at the beginning of each unit to help you set goals, plan your time, and keep track of the work you do.

IN THIS UNIT, YOU WILL LEARN HOW TO

Each unit begins with an overview of the language you will be learning and skills you will be acquiring.

MY PROGRESS TRACKER

Use the progress tracker to plan your study time and to keep a record of what you've accomplished. The first column tracks time, and the remaining five columns represent the skills you'll be working on: listening, pronunciation, reading, writing, and spoken interaction.

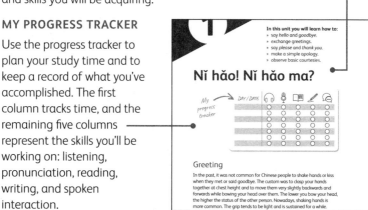

Personalize the tracker: Instead of the date or day, you can enter an increment of time (15 minutes, 1 hour...). Add columns for culture, vocabulary, grammar or any other area you wish to focus on. Give yourself a star when you feel you've done particularly well. Make it your own! Review your tracker regularly and see which areas could use more practice.

Use the **Self check** at the end of each unit to evaluate your progress.

How the book works   ix

Try to practise each skill every day.

The icons in the progress tracker are used throughout the book to help you easily identify and locate the skills you want to practice:

 Listening practice

 Pronunciation practice

 Reading

 Writing

 Speaking – conversation skills

Remember: there are many ways to build your skills in addition to those provided in this book: use a language-learning app, listen to music or podcasts, watch TV shows or movies, go to a restaurant, follow Chinese social media accounts (there are wonderful teachers who post regularly), read blogs, newspapers or magazines, switch the language settings in your apps to Mandarin Chinese or sign up for a language exchange or a tutor.

UNITS 1–10

Each unit in *Beginners' Mandarin Chinese* is structured in the following way:

- ▶ **Culture point** presents an interesting cultural aspect related to the unit theme, introduces some key words and phrases and includes a challenging question for you.
- ▶ **Vocabulary builder** introduces key unit vocabulary grouped by theme and conversations, and is accompanied by audio. Learn these words and you will be on your way to speaking fluent Chinese.
- ▶ **Conversations** are recorded dialogues you can listen to and practise, beginning with a narrative that helps you understand what you will hear, a focusing question and follow-up activities.
- ▶ **Language discovery** draws your attention to key language points in the conversations, whether it is a grammar rule or a way of saying things. Read the notes and look at the conversations to see how the language is used in practice and to aid quicker learning.

- **Practice** offers a variety of exercises, including speaking opportunities, to give you a chance to 'pull it all together' and make active use of the language.
- **Speaking and listening** offers copious practice in speaking and understanding Chinese through exercises that let you use what you have learned in the unit and previously. Try to do the Speaking activity spontaneously. The Listening activities increase your understanding of spoken Chinese.
- **Reading and writing** provides practice in reading everyday items and contains mostly vocabulary from the unit. Try getting the gist of the text before you answer the follow-up questions.
- **Test yourself** and the **Vocabulary and Pronunciation** exercises help you assess what you have learned. Do the tests without looking at the text.
- **Self check** lets you see what you can do in Chinese after mastering each unit. When you feel confident that you can use the language correctly, move on to the next unit.

Study the units at your own pace, and remember to make frequent and repeated use of the audio.

As you work your way through the course, you will also become familiar with studying on your own, looking things up and checking your Chinese language ability.

Here are some resources you can always consult:

- **Useful expressions** provides a quick reference for everyday phrases and numbers.
- **Pronunciation guide** overviews Mandarin Chinese sounds. We encourage you to practise pronunciation as you begin the course and go over it regularly. You can find the guide at the beginning of the book.
- **The Chinese writing system** – this section introduces Chinese characters and teaches you how to write the language. Start with this and don't be afraid to spend some significant time absorbing the information given. You will find this section at the beginning of the book. By reading and absorbing this, you will be better placed to understand the key characters section at the end of each unit. In each unit you will find at least one useful sign written in Chinese

characters (**Hànzì**) so you can familiarize yourself with what they look like even though you haven't actually learnt any characters.

There are two major reviews in addition to the **Test yourself** and **Vocabulary and Pronunciation** exercises at the end of each unit: after Unit 5 and after Unit 10. Your score will let you know if you are ready to move ahead or if you should go back and refresh your knowledge.

At the back of the book is a reference section:

▶ **Answer key** helps you monitor your performance and check your progress. The Answer key includes answers to all the activities in the main teaching unit and also to those in the review units. Do remember that variations are possible in some of the answers but we couldn't include them all.

▶ **Chinese–English vocabulary** allows you to quickly access the vocabulary that is presented in the course.

▶ **English–Chinese vocabulary** lists the most useful words you will need when expressing yourself in Chinese. Please note that many of the words in the vocabulary have not appeared in the dialogues. The list is provided as a convenient companion for your reference.

▶ **Appendix**: character texts offer the Chinese character version of all the dialogues. By all means use it to help you on your way as you learn the Chinese writing system but it will be a challenge too far at this stage to try and use it to read the language. Instead, constantly practise reading the **pīnyīn** romanization.

Soon you will be speaking Mandarin Chinese – a language spoken by around 1 billion other people as their first language, of a country with one of the world's strongest economies and a rich, diverse culture still largely unknown in the West.

Mandarin Chinese is one of the fastest growing spoken languages in the world in terms of numbers and is also one of the official languages of the UN.

You will find it both entertaining and fulfilling. So, good luck and have fun!

Learn to learn

The Discovery method

There are lots of approaches to language learning, some practical, some quite unconventional. Perhaps you know of a few, or even have some techniques of your own. In this book we have incorporated the **Discovery method** of learning, a sort of DIY approach to language learning. What this means is that you will be encouraged throughout the course to engage your mind and figure out the language for yourself, through identifying patterns, understanding grammar concepts, noticing words that are similar to English and more.

Simply put, if you figure something out for yourself, you're more likely to understand it. And when you use what you've learned, you're more likely to remember it. And because many of the essential but (let's admit it!) dull details, such as grammar rules, are introduced through the **Discovery method**, you'll have more fun while learning. Soon, the language will start to make sense and you'll be relying on your own intuition to construct original sentences independently, not just listening and repeating.

Enjoy yourself!

Be a successful language learner!

There are many strategies that can help you become a successful language learner. Different people have different learning styles and some of these approaches will be more effective for you than others. Use this list as a point of inspiration when you want to find the most effective ways to advance your skills and begin your journey to fluency.

VOCABULARY

Words are the building blocks of language. The more you use the words you're introduced to, the more quickly they'll lodge into your memory. These study tips will help you remember better:

▶ Group new words under **generic categories** such as *family members* or *food*; **situations** in which they occur such as *for asking directions: crossroads, traffic lights, left, right, bus stop*; and functions such as *greetings, parting, thanks, apologizing*.

- Write the words over and over. Keep lists on your phone or tablet, or in a notebook.
- Listen to the audio several times and say the words out loud as you hear or read them.
- Cover up English translations and try to remember the meanings. Cover up romanizations and pronounce the words on your own.
- Create flash cards, drawings and mind maps.
- Write Chinese words on sticky notes and stick them to objects around your house.
- Look for patterns in words, for example adding **měi** to a word means *every*, so **měi tiān** means *every day*, **měi xīngqī** means *every week*, **měi yuè** means *every month*, **měi nián** means *every year*, etc.
- Experiment with words. Use words in new contexts and find out if they are correct.

GRAMMAR

Grammar gives your language structure. It allows you to experiment with the vocabulary you learn because you'll understand how they work together to create meaning. In other words, you'll begin to develop a feel for the language. Here are some tips to help you study more effectively:
- Write your own grammar glossary and add new information and examples as you go along.
- Reflect on how the rules of Chinese compare with your own language or other languages you may speak.
- Try to find rules and be ready to spot the exceptions. By doing this, you'll remember the rules better and get a feel for the language.
- Try to find examples of grammar in conversations or other articles.
- Keep a 'pattern bank' of examples for structures you've learned.
- Experiment with the rules. Use known vocabulary to practise new grammar structures.

PRONUNCIATION

The best way to improve your pronunciation is simply to practice as much as possible:
- Keep a list of the words that give you trouble. Practise them separately.
- Repeat all of the conversations, line by line. Listen to yourself and try to mimic what you hear.

- Record yourself and compare yourself to the recordings.
- Study individual sounds, then full words.
- Don't forget, it's not just about pronouncing letters and words correctly, but using the right tone and intonation. So, when practising, mimic the rising and falling intonation of Mandarin speakers.

LISTENING AND READING

The conversations in this book include questions to help guide you in your understanding. But you can go further by following some of these tips.

- **Imagine the situation.** Try to imagine the scenes and make educated guesses about the topic and vocabulary – a conversation in a café is likely to be about drinks or food.
- **Get the gist.** Concentrate on the main part and don't worry about individual words.
- **Guess the meaning of key words.** Use the context and your own experience or knowledge of the topic to guess the sorts of words in a reading passage or dialogue.

SPEAKING

The greatest obstacle to speaking a new language is the fear of making a mistake. Keep in mind that you make mistakes in your own language – it's simply part of the human condition. Accept it. Focus on the message. Most errors are not serious and they will not affect the meaning. Concentrate on getting your message across and use the mistakes as learning opportunities.

Here are some useful tips to help you start speaking:

- Rehearse in Chinese. Hold a conversation with yourself using the conversations of the units as models and the structures you have learned previously.
- After you have conducted a transaction with a sales assistant, server, etc. in your own language, pretend that you have to do it in Chinese, e.g. buying groceries, ordering food and drinks, and so on.
- Look at objects around you and try to name them in Chinese.
- Look at people around you and try to describe them in detail.
- Try to answer all of the questions in the book out loud.

Learn to learn

- ▶ Say the dialogues out loud then try to replace sentences with ones that are true for you.
- ▶ Try to role-play different situations in the book.

WRITING

Explore the section on the Chinese writing system at the beginning of the book, and familiarize yourself with the characters introduced at the end of each unit.

Learning a language takes work. But the work can be a lot of fun! So, let's begin!

WHAT DO YOU DO IF YOU DON'T UNDERSTAND?

1 Don't panic and don't give up listening.

2 Try to concentrate on what you do understand and guess the rest. If there comes a point where you really feel you can't understand anything, isolate the phrase or word(s) that is causing you problems and say to the speaker:

| **. . . shì shénme yìsi?** | *What does . . . mean?* |

Hopefully they will say it in another way that you will be able to understand. If not, here are two useful sentences:

| **Qǐng nǐ zài shuō yí biàn.** | *Please say it again.* |
| **Qǐng nǐ shuō màn yìdiǎn.** | *Please speak more slowly.* |

The Mandarin language

GRAMMAR: THE ESSENTIALS

The fundamental building block of the Chinese language is the character, a single-syllable morpheme whereby each individual character forms one idea. And there are in the region of 400 of these basic monosyllables in Chinese – when these individual 'cells' of the language are combined, they form homophones, in which Chinese abounds. Unfortunately, this is what adds to the complicated nature of the language. This difficulty (for us as learners of Chinese) is ameliorated somewhat by Chinese being a tonal language. **Pǔtōnghuà** (Mandarin) has four tones, so our original paltry 400-odd monosyllables become over 1400 different sounds (as some sound plus tone combinations do not exist) in one fell swoop. But also the characters that we find combined in this way have similar meanings when used to form the new 'word' – confusion here is avoided since, when used separately, individual characters may take on another meaning but in combination, they can usually only mean one thing.

Most syllables in Chinese consist of two elements: an initial and a final, the former being a consonant at the beginning of the syllable and the latter the rest of the syllable.

INITIALS

There are some 21 initials in Modern Standard Chinese (often abbreviated to MSC), which is what you will be learning on this course. The semi-vowels **w** and **y** are considered by some to be initials, too. In addition, there is **ng**, a sound that occurs at the end of a syllable, as the same sound does in English. This sound includes six aspirated initials and six unaspirated initials, all 12 of which are voiceless. When making an aspirated sound, a feather or a sheet of paper held in front of your mouth will move; when making an unaspirated one, it should not. Lack of vibration in your vocal cords renders the initial voiceless.

FINALS

Chinese has 36 finals, which are composed of a simple or compound vowel or a vowel plus a nasal consonant. Some syllables may lack the initial consonant but none lacks a vowel.

TONES

The four tones in Chinese (remember that their presence multiplies the number of possible sounds available to about 1400) are variations in pitch – rising, continuing and falling. Each syllable in the language has its own specific tone, so they are an important component in 'word' formation.

The first tone is high and level, the second is rising, the third tone is a short fall followed by a rising tone and the fourth tone is a falling tone. (Note, however, that you do not have to produce a particular sort of sound in your own speech – all the tones occur naturally within the voice range.)

There is also a neutral tone, i.e. the syllable is toneless: all particles are neutral, the second half of a repeated word may be in neutral tone, fill-in syllables are neutral and the second syllable in a compound may be neutral (but on other occasions, not, so this neutrality has to be indicated in the text). One example is **xièxie**, *thank you*.

In the spoken language, you will find that it is rare for tones to be given their full value, but this doesn't let you off the hook! You should still learn them as if they were and, also, be aware that learning the words with their tone takes time, practice and lots of listening and repetition on your part. So do persevere!

SOME ADDITIONAL POINTS

Here are a couple of extra points, which are helpful to note as you embark on this course:

▶ One way in which to ask questions in Chinese is to use both positive and negative forms of the verb together. And then the corresponding answer is neither yes nor no but either the positive or negative form of that verb.

▶ As you know by now, Chinese does not have a phonetic alphabet and **pīnyīn** is the nearest we in the West get to a recognizable form of transcribing it. It will be very useful for you in this course, as it provides a relatively accurate guide to correct pronunciation.

▶ Where names in the West appear in the form title, given name, surname, in Chinese, they appear entirely the other way around, i.e. surname, given name, title. Hence in the name Mao Zedong, Mao was the Chinese leader's surname and Zedong was actually his given name.

- ▶ Some adjectives function as verbs, a form known as *stative* verbs, meaning that, when using a *to be* verb with an adjective, there is no need to actually say *to be*.
- ▶ Unlike in English, an adverb will always go in front of the verb it is qualifying.
- ▶ One feature of the language that should please you immensely (especially if you have learnt other languages in the past or if English is not your first language and you have had to struggle with this aspect) is that all verbs are invariable – meaning that they remain exactly the same, no matter what else is going on! Another feature of verbs that you will like is that (with one exception – the verb *to have* **yǒu**), negation comes through the use of **bù**, which precedes the verb.

We hope that this short introduction has kindled your interest and that you enjoy the course.

Abbreviations

(sing.) singular   (lit.) literally
(pl.)   plural   (MW)   measure word

Punctuation

Chinese punctuation is very similar to that of English but a pause-mark (、) is used in lists instead of a comma, even if the list only has two items in it. A comma is used for longer pauses.

Use of the apostrophe

An apostrophe (') is used to show where the break comes between two syllables if there is any possible ambiguity in pronunciation, for example, **shí'èr** (not **shíèr**), **nǚ'ér** (not **nǚér**).

Use of hyphens

We have used hyphens to show how words are built up in Chinese:

Zhōngguó *China* + **rén** *person* → **Zhōngguó-rén** *a Chinese person*
Déguó *Germany* + **rén** → **Déguó-rén** *a German person*

A hyphen is also used to link a verbal suffix or verbal complement to the verb. This will encourage you to say it together with the verb as it should be said:

Wǒ chī-guo Yìndù fàn.   *I've eaten Indian food.*
Tā méi qù-guo Zhōngguó.   *He's never been to China.*
Nǐ shuō-de hěn màn.   *You speak very slowly.*
Tāmen xiě-de bú kuài.   *They don't write quickly.*

In general, we have written 'words' separately except where they are seen as being one idea:

hǎo	*good*	but	**hǎo deduō**	*much better*
tā	*he, she, it*	but	**tāde**	*his, hers, its*
xīngqī	*week*	but	**xīngqīyī**	*Monday*
yuè	*month*	but	**yīyuè**	*January*
běn	*measure word for books*	but	**běnzi**	*notebook*

However, verb-objects and so on are separate for clarity:

shuō (verb) **huà** (object)   *to speak* (speech)
shuō Fǎyǔ   *to speak French*

Pronunciation guide

 00.01 TONES

Chinese is a tonal language. Every syllable in Chinese has its own tone. **Pǔtōnghuà** has four distinct tones plus a neutral tone. This means that syllables which are pronounced the same but have different tones will mean different things. For example, **tang** pronounced in the first tone means *soup* but pronounced in the second tone means *sugar*! But don't worry – all the four tones fall within your natural voice range. You don't have to have a particular type of voice to speak Chinese.

The four tones are represented by the following marks which are put over the vowel, such as **nǐ** *you* or over the main vowel of a syllable where there are two or three vowels, for example, **hǎo** *good*, **guó** *country*:

- ¯ 1st tone, high and level
- ´ 2nd tone, rising
- ˇ 3rd tone, falling – rising
- ` 4th tone, falling

The following diagrams will help to make this clearer.

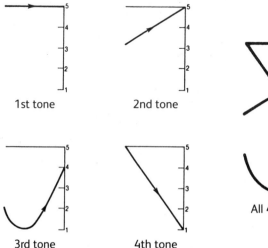

1st tone   2nd tone

3rd tone   4th tone

All 4 tones together

Think of 1 as being at the bottom of your voice range and 5 at the top.

1st tone: Pitch it where you feel comfortable. Say *oo* as in *zoo* and keep going for as long as you can. You should be able to keep it up for maybe half a minute. When you have got used to that, change to another vowel sound and practise that in the same way and so on.

2nd tone: Raise your eyebrows every time you attempt a second tone until you get used to it. This is infallible!

3rd tone: Drop your chin onto your neck and raise it again. Then practise the sound doing the movement at the same time.

4th tone: Stamp your foot gently and then accompany this action with the relevant sound.

Neutral tone: Some syllables in Chinese are toneless or occur in the neutral tone. This means they have no tone mark over the vowel. They are rather like unstressed syllables in English, such as 'of a' in 'two of a kind'.

TONE CHANGES

Occasionally syllables may change their tones.

Two 3rd tones, one after another, are very difficult to say. Where this happens, the first one is said as a 2nd tone. We have still marked it as a 3rd tone in the book otherwise you may think that it is always a 2nd tone, which it isn't:

Nǐ hǎo! (*How do you do?*) is said as **Ní hǎo**.

If three 3rd tones occur together, the first two are normally said as 2nd tones:

Wǒ yě hǎo (*I'm OK too*) is said as **Wó yé hǎo**.

Note that in the phrase **yí ge rén** (one [measure word] person), the **ge** is said without a tone although it is actually 4th, but it still carries enough weight to change the **yì** into a 2nd tone.

You will find a few other tone changes in the book. These will be pointed out to you when they occur for the first time.

Listen to the tones and copy the pronunciation of the speaker.

00.02 CHINESE SOUNDS

Vowels

Here is a list of the Chinese vowels with a rough English equivalent sound and then one or two examples in Chinese. There are single vowels, compound vowels and vowels plus a nasal sound, which will be listed separately.

	Rough English sound	Chinese examples
a	*father*	**baba, mama**
ai	*bite*	**tai, zai**
ao	*cow*	**hao, zhao**
e	*fur*	**che, he, ge**
ei	*play*	**bei, gei, shei, fei**
i	*tea*	**didi, feiji, ni**
i (after z, c, s, zh, ch, sh and r only)		**zi, ci, shi**

The **i** is there more or less for cosmetic reasons – no syllable can exist without a vowel. Say the consonant and 'sit on it' and you have the sound.

ia	*yarrow*	**jia, xia**
iao	*meow*	**biao, piao, yao**
ie	*yes*	**bie, xie, ye**
iu	*yo-yo*	**liu, jiu, you**

y replaces **i** at the beginning of a word if there is no initial consonant.

o	*more*	**moyimo, mapo**
ou	*go*	**dou, zou**
u	*moo*	**bu, zhu**
ua	*suave*	**gua, hua**
uo	*war*	**shuo, cuo, wo**
uai	*swipe*	**kuai, wai**
ui	*weigh*	**dui, gui, zui**

w replaces **u** at the beginning of a word if there is no initial consonant.

ü	*pneumonia*	**ju, qu, lü, nü**
üe	*pneumatic + air* (said quickly)	**yue, xue, jue**

Note that **ü** and **üe** can occur only with the consonants **n**, **l**, **j**, **q** and **x**. As **j**, **q** and **x** cannot occur as **j+u**, **q+u** or **x+u**, the umlaut (¨) over the **u** in **ju**, **qu** and **xu** has been omitted. **N** and **l**, however, can occur as both **nu** and **nü**, **lu** and **lü** so the umlaut has been kept.

Yu replaces **ü**, and **yue** replaces **üe** if there is no initial consonant.

Here are the vowels with a nasal sound formed with vowels followed by **n** or **ng**. Speak through your nose when you pronounce them and listen carefully to the audio.

Pronunciation guide

	Rough English sound	Chinese examples
an	*man*	fan, man
ang	*bang*	zhang, shang
en	*under*	ren, hen
eng	*hung*	deng, neng
in	*bin*	nin, jin, xin
ian	*yen*	tian, nian, qian
iang	*Yangtse (River)*	liang, xiang
ing	*finger*	ming, qing, xing
iong	*Jung* (the psychoanalyst)	yong, qiong, xiong
ong	*Jung* (the psychoanalyst)	tong, cong, hong
uan	*wangle*	wan, suan, huan
un	*won*	wen, lun, chun
uang	*wrong*	wang, huang, zhuang
üan	*pneumatic + end* (said quickly)	yuan, quan, xuan
ün	'une' in French	yun, jun, qun

Note that **ian** is pronounced **yen**.

The same rules about **y** replacing **i** and **w** replacing **u** at the beginning of a word if there is no initial consonant also apply to vowels with a nasal sound.

Yuan replaces **üan** and **yun** replaces **ün** if there is no initial consonant.

CONSONANTS

Here is a list of the Chinese consonants, some of which are quite similar to English sounds, others less so. Those that are very different from the nearest English sound are explained.

	Rough English sound	Chinese examples
b	*bore*	bai, bei
p	*poor*	pao, pang
m	*me*	ma, mei, ming
f	*fan*	fan, feng
d	*door*	da, dou, duo
t	*tore*	ta, tai, tian
n	*need*	na, nü, nian
l	*lie*	lai, lei, liang
z	*adds*	zi, zai, zuo
c	*its*	ci, cai, cuo
s	*say*	si, sui, suan

The next four consonants are all made with the tongue loosely rolled in the middle of the mouth.

zh	*jelly*	**zhao, zhong, zhu**
ch	*chilly*	**che, chi, chang**
sh	*shy*	**shi, shei, sheng**
r	*razor*	**re, ri, rong**

The next three consonants are all made with the tongue flat and the corners of the mouth drawn back as far as possible.

j	*genius*	**jia, jiao, jian**
q	*cheese* (as said in front of the camera!)	**qi, qian, qu**
x	*sheet* (rather like a whistling kettle)	**xiao, xin, xue**

Arch the back of the tongue towards the roof of the mouth for the last three consonants.

g	*guard*	**ge, gei, gui**
k	*card*	**kai, kan, kuai**
h	*loch*	**he, huan, hao**

LEARNING TIPS TO HELP YOUR PRONUNCIATION

1 Go back to the Pronunciation guide and read the notes again. The best way of learning this selection of sounds is in pairs, as follows:

b and **p**   **zh** and **ch**
d and **t**   **j** and **q**
z and **c**   **g** and **k**

2 Take a sheet of A4 paper and hold it vertically in front of you. Say **b** . . . If you are saying it correctly the sheet will not move. Then say **p** and the top of the sheet should be blown away from you. The same should happen with **d** and **t**, i.e. the sheet should not move when you say **d** but it should move with **t**! Repeat this with each remaining pair. The sheet should not move with **z**, **zh**, **j** and **g** but it should move with **c**, **ch**, **q** and **k**.

3 Here are two more pairs: **lu** and **lü**, **nu** and **nü**.

Go back to the Pronunciation guide and read the notes there. You will need a mirror for the next exercise.

First of all push out your lips and say *oo*. Then tighten them and say *you*. Repeat this but put *l* in front of the *oo*. Now you have the sound **lu**. To say **lü** say the word *lewd* without the *d*. For **nu** and **nü** say the *noo* of *noodles* and the *nu* of *nude*! Now look in the mirror and say the sounds again. What do you notice about your lips when you say the two different sounds?

You have to tighten them to say the **ü** sound, don't you? For those of you who know a little French or German, the **ü** in Chinese is like the *u* in *tu* (French) or the *ü* in *über* (German).

ju, **qu** and **xu** are also pronounced as though they were written with **ü**. Don't confuse them with **zhu**, **chu** and **shu** where the **u** is the *oo* sound.

4 Here's another set of pairs:

j and **q**
zh and **ch**
sh and **r**

Go back to the Pronunciation guide again and read the notes there.

The **j** in Chinese is the same as our own. Say *jeans*, in the same way as you would say *cheese* to the camera, a few times and observe your mouth in a mirror. You will notice that the corners of your mouth are drawn back as far as they can go.

Q bears no resemblance to our *q*. It is pronounced in exactly the same way as **j** but you put air behind it to make the **q**.

For **zh**, **ch**, **sh** and **r** you must curl your tongue back in a loose sausage roll. They are all pronounced with the tongue in this position. **Zh** and **ch** are identical sounds except the **ch** is said with air behind it.

R is the one to watch. Listen to the audio carefully and try to reproduce the sounds you hear as closely as possible. Recording your own voice and then comparing it with the original would be extremely helpful at this stage.

Useful expressions

00.03 GREETINGS, FAREWELLS AND COURTESIES

hello	**nǐ hǎo**
goodbye	**zàijiàn**
see you tomorrow	**míngtiān jiàn**
how are you?	**nǐ hǎo ma?**
yes	**shì** (*it is*); **duì** (*it's correct*)
no	**bú shì** (*it's not*); **bú duì** (*it's incorrect*)
please	**qǐng**
thank you	**xièxie (nǐ)**
you're welcome (it's OK)	**bú kèqi**
excuse me	**duìbuqǐ**
sorry	**duìbuqǐ**
cheers	**gānbēi**
(to) your good health	**zhù nǐ shēntǐ jiànkāng**
bon voyage	**(zhù nǐ) yí lù píng'ān**

00.04 MAKING YOURSELF UNDERSTOOD

please repeat that	**qǐng zài shuō yí biàn**
please speak slowly	**qǐng shuō màn yìdiǎn**
I don't understand	**wǒ bù dǒng**
I understand	**wǒ dǒng**
I don't speak Chinese	**wǒ bú huì shuō Zhōngwén**

00.05 QUESTION WORDS

where?	**nǎr?, nǎli?**
how?	**zěnme?**
when?	**shénme shíhou?**
how much?	**duōshao?**
why?	**wèishénme?**
who?	**shuí?, shéi?**

Useful expressions

00.06 NUMBERS 0–10

0	líng	零 / 〇
1	yī	一
2	èr	二
3	sān	三
4	sì	四
5	wǔ	五
6	liù	六
7	qī	七
8	bā	八
9	jiǔ	九
10	shí	十

00.07 NUMBERS 11–100

11	shíyī	十一
12	shí'èr	十二
13	shísān	十三
14	shísì	十四
15	shíwǔ	十五
16	shíliù	十六
17	shíqī	十七
18	shíbā	十八
19	shíjiǔ	十九
20	èrshí	二十
30	sānshí	三十
40	sìshí	四十
50	wǔshí	五十
60	liùshí	六十
70	qīshí	七十
80	bāshí	八十
90	jiǔshí	九十
100	yìbǎi	一百
1000	yìqiān	一千

00.08 MONTHS

January	**yīyuè**
February	**èryuè**
March	**sānyuè**
April	**sìyuè**
May	**wǔyuè**
June	**liùyuè**
July	**qīyuè**
August	**bāyuè**
September	**jiǔyuè**
October	**shíyuè**
November	**shíyīyuè**
December	**shí'èryuè**

00.09 DAYS OF THE WEEK

Monday	**xīngqīyī**
Tuesday	**xīngqī'èr**
Wednesday	**xīngqīsān**
Thursday	**xīngqīsì**
Friday	**xīngqīwǔ**
Saturday	**xīngqīliù**
Sunday	**xīngqītiān** (or **xīngqīrì**)

00.10 POINTS OF THE COMPASS

(In the order in which Chinese people normally say them)

east	**dōng**
south	**nán**
west	**xī**
north	**běi**
southeast	**dōngnán**
southwest	**xīnán**
northeast	**dōngběi**
northwest	**xīběi**

Useful expressions

The written language

WŎMEN KÀNKAN HÀNZÌ BA!
LET'S LOOK AT CHINESE CHARACTERS!

Contrary to what most people believe, Chinese is not a difficult language to speak – particularly at beginner's level. Pronunciation and grammar are generally straightforward even if they require you to do a few things you're not used to. Even tones are not intrinsically difficult and can be fun, though they do involve a lot of time and practice.

Nobody can say, however, that learning to read and write Chinese characters is easy – fascinating, yes, but not easy. That is why we have written this book in **pīnyīn**, so that the learner can get straight down to speaking Chinese without the barrier of an unknown form of writing.

What follows is a special section designed to give you the chance to find out something about the origin of Chinese characters and to have a taste of what's involved in reading and writing them. This section is designed as a 'one-off' so that those of you who would rather concentrate solely on listening and speaking can miss it out without it affecting your understanding of the units which follow.

In this section you will be introduced to the Chinese writing system and learn:

The structure of Chinese characters.

The rules of writing.

How to write the numbers 1–99.

How to write the days of the week and the date.

How to write the time.

BEFORE YOU START

You will remember from the introduction that this section is independent of the rest of the book, so if you have decided not to get involved with the Chinese script, you can miss it out. Alternatively, you can choose to come back to it later when you have finished the other units. Even if you don't do any of the exercises in this section, it would be a good idea to read it through, so that at least you have some idea of what the Chinese script is all about. This will help your understanding of the Chinese language as a whole and hence of the people who speak it.

THE CHINESE WRITING SYSTEM

Chinese characters (**Hànzì**) are the symbols used to write the Chinese language. Written Chinese does not use a phonetic alphabet. This means that you cannot guess how a character (**zì**) is pronounced just by looking at it. The Chinese script is extremely old. Its earliest written records date back over 3500 years. These are the markings on oracle bones (tortoise shells and animal bones) on which the priests used to scratch their questions to the gods. The earliest characters were pictures representing easily recognizable objects, such as the sun, the moon, fire, water, a mountain, a tree, and so on.

Such characters (**zì**) were known as pictographs. Some of them are still in use even today.

The next step was for pictographs to be combined to form new characters, known as ideographs because they express an idea:

日 *sun* + 月 *moon* = 明 *bright*
女 *woman* + 子 *child* = 好 *good*
日 *sun* + 木 *tree* = 東 *east* (the sun coming up behind a tree)
人 *person* + 木 *tree* = 休 *to rest* (a person leaning up against a tree)

So far so good! Unfortunately, only a limited number of ideas could be expressed in this way so then characters were created which contained a meaning element (often known as the radical) and a phonetic element which was to help with the pronunciation of the character. Of course, pronunciation has changed over the centuries, so that now this phonetic element is only of limited help. Let's look at a few of these radical-phonetic or compound characters. You can see how such characters came into being and what they look like today.

Both the characters to the right are pronounced the same, although they have different tones. This is quite normal. The next pair have the same pronunciation and the same tone, but this is unusual.

fēn *divide; separate*   **fěn** *powder*

The written language

lǐ *village; mile; inside*   **lǐ** *polish; reason; principle*

At the opposite end of the spectrum we have the following three characters, which have a common phonetic element 母 **mu**, but are pronounced quite differently. This is the worst scenario!

mǔ *mother*   **měi** *every*   **hǎi** *sea*

THE BASIC RULES FOR WRITING CHINESE CHARACTERS

As you can imagine, there are some basic rules for writing Chinese characters which you need to master. This is important if you are to remember them, and so the brain needs to operate a kind of orderly filing system. To do this, it needs help. Chinese characters should always be written the same way, so that they become fixed in your imaginary filing system. Most characters are made up of two or more basic structural parts called 'character components', although of course some character components such as 日 **rì** (*sun*) can stand by themselves, as we mentioned earlier. Although the total number of characters is quite large, the number of character components is limited. These components are written with a number of basic strokes, which are illustrated here:

Stroke	Name	
丶	diǎn	*dot*
一	héng	*horizontal*
丨	shù	*vertical*
丿	piě	*left-falling*
乀	nà	*right-falling*
⼂	tí	*rising*
亅 乚 𠄌	gōu	*hook*
⼉	zhé	*turning*

These strokes are basically straight lines and were traditionally written in ink with a hair brush. The main directions are from top to bottom and from left to right. The arrows on the basic strokes opposite show how the characters are written by indicating the direction each stroke takes:

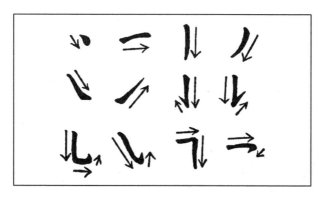

The rules of stroke order in writing Chinese characters and character components are as follows:

Example	Stroke order					Rule
十	一				十	First horizontal, then vertical
人	丿				人	First left-falling, then right-falling
三	一	二			三	From top to bottom
州	丶	丿	丬	州 州	州	From left to right
月	丿	冂	月		月	First outside, then inside
四	丨	冂	匹	四	四	Finish inside, then close
小	亅		小		小	Middle, then the two sides

The written language xxxiii

Numbers 1–10

Now let's try writing the numbers 1 to 10. We have shown the direction and sequence of each stroke to help you. It is helpful to think of each character, however simple or complex, as occupying a square of the same size.

Numbers 11–99

11 is 10 + 1   = 十一
12 is 10 + 2   = 十二
20 is 2 × 10   = 二十
30 is 3 × 10   = 三十
65 is 6 × 10 + 5 = 六十五
99 is 9 × 10 + 9 = 九十九

It is worth noting that Arabic numerals are being used more and more in China. Newspapers and magazines in the People's Republic all use Arabic numerals for dates and (large) numbers. The traditional Chinese characters are still widely used in Hong Kong and Taiwan.

PRACTICE

1 Which numbers do the following characters represent?

a 二
b 六
c 十
d 五
e 十一
f 二十四
g 八十三
h 六十九
i 五十七
j 三十六

2 Write out the following numbers in Chinese characters:

a 3
b 8
c 10
d 15
e 42
f 98
g 67

(The answers to all the exercises are in the Answer key at the back of the book.)

xxxiv

DAYS OF THE WEEK

All you need to know to write the characters for the days of the week are the two characters **xīng** (*star*) and **qī** (*period*) which, when combined together, form the word for week; plus the numbers 1 to 6 and the characters for *sun* (**rì**) or *day* (**tiān**). **Xīng** is made up of the radical 日 **rì** (*sun*) and 生 **shēng** (*to give birth*):

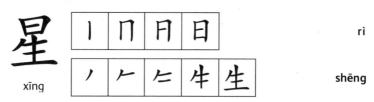

Qī is made up of the phonetic element 其 **qí** and the radical 月 **yuè** (*moon*).

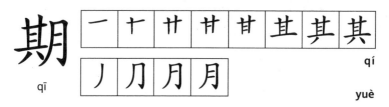

You have already met 日 **rì** (*sun*).

Tiān (*day*) is also a nice easy character:

It is actually made up of one horizontal stroke plus the character 大 **dà** (*big*).

Revise the days of the week and then do the following exercises.

The written language

PRACTICE

3 Which day of the week . . .

  a comes after Saturday? 星期 ☐

  b comes after Tuesday? 星期 ☐

  c are many football matches played in the UK? 星期 ☐

  d comes before Friday? 星期 ☐

4 Now fill in the missing characters for the days of the week:

  a Sunday   星期 ☐ or 星期 ☐

  b Tuesday   星 ☐ 二

  c Friday   星 ☐ 五

  d Thursday ☐ 期四

  e Saturday ☐ 期六

HOW TO WRITE THE DATE

For this you need to revise your numbers (1–31) and the characters for moon or month (**yuè** 月). Having done that, check up on how to say the date in Chinese (see Unit 5). In formal written Chinese **rì** 日 is used instead of **hào** 号. Thus, 21 February is:

二月二十一日   èryuè èrshíyī rì

Practice

5 Can you recognize the following dates?
  a 十一月三日
  b 六月十八日
  c 七月十一日
  d 十月十四日
  e 八月二十九日

xxxvi

6 Can you write out the following dates in Chinese characters?

   a Christmas Day (25 December)

   | | | | | | | |

   b International Women's Day (8 March)

   | | | |

   c Your birthday (you might not fill all the squares in!)

   | | | | | | | |

   d Your father's birthday

   | | | | | | | |

   e Your mother's birthday

   | | | | | | |

HOW TO WRITE THE YEARS

This is very easy! You will get more practice on this in Unit 5 (Language discovery 2).

1945 is 一九四五 **nián** (*year*).

Nián is written:

年 | ノ | ㇇ | ⸍ | ㇏ | ㇓ | 年

PRACTICE

7 Write down the years represented by the Chinese characters in the spaces provided:

e.g.	一九一四年	_1914_
a	二〇〇*八年	_____
b	一九三七年	_____
c	一九四九年	_____
d	一八八五年	_____
e	一六四二年	_____

* 〇 is used for zero in the People's Republic of China while the traditional character 零 **líng** is still widely used in Hong Kong and Taiwan.

HOW TO WRITE THE TIME

For this you will need to learn to write the character for *minute* **fēn** 分 and the characters for *o'clock* **diǎn** (**zhōng**). Before you do this, revise how to tell the time (Unit 5). Now let's look at the two characters **diǎn** and **zhōng**.

点
diǎn

is made up of the radical for fire **huǒ** ⺣ (also written 火) and the phonetic element 占 **zhàn**. Whoops! This one has moved a long way from its original pronunciation. **Diǎn** is written as follows:

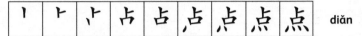 diǎn

钟
zhōng

is made up of the radical for *metal* **jīn** 钅 (also written 金) and the phonetic element 中 **zhōng**. Whew! This character is **zhōng** too! **Zhōng** is written as follows:

 zhōng

So **3.20** is 三点二十分 and **5.00** is 五点钟

By the way, you should never give a Chinese person a clock for a present, as the character for *clock* has exactly the same sound and tone (**zhōng**) as the character in classical Chinese meaning *the end* or *death*. So giving somebody a clock might send the wrong message!

You will also need to know the characters for *quarter* **kè**, for *half* **bàn**, and for *minus* or *to lack* **chà**.

kè

is made up of the radical for *knife* **dāo** 刂 (also written 刀) and the phonetic element 亥 **hài**. **Kè** is written as follows:

 kè

bàn

is made up of the vertical line radical | and the phonetic element 八 **bā** (often written ⺍ as here), plus two horizontal lines. **Bàn** is written as follows:

 bàn

chà

is made up of the radical for *sheep* **yáng** 羊 (slanted here) and the phonetic element 工 **gōng**. No help here for pronunciation, unfortunately. **Chà** is written as follows:

 chà

PRACTICE

8 What time is it?

    a 九点一刻   9.15
    b 十二点二十五分
    c 六点半
    d 差十分四点
    e 八点差一刻

9 Can you write out the following times in Chinese characters? (One square represents one Chinese character, but there are alternatives.)

    a 6.20
    b 11.45
    c 10.10
    d 4.48
    e 7.30

Congratulations! If you have got this far you obviously have an aptitude for writing and recognizing Chinese characters. Hopefully, some of the key characters at the end of each unit will also make a bit more sense to you.

The different style of writing Chinese characters is an art form known as calligraphy, which is highly valued by the Chinese. You have just had a little taste of it!

If you have enjoyed learning something about Chinese characters, why not go on to *Read and Write Chinese Script*, which will allow you to explore the Chinese script even more?

1

In this unit you will learn how to:
» say *hello* and *goodbye*.
» exchange greetings.
» say *please* and *thank you*.
» make a simple apology.
» observe basic courtesies.

Nǐ hǎo! Nǐ hǎo ma?

My progress tracker

Greeting

In the past, it was not common for Chinese people to shake hands or kiss when they met or said goodbye. The custom was to clasp your hands together at chest height and to move them very slightly backwards and forwards while bowing your head over them. The lower you bow your head, the higher the status of the other person. Nowadays, shaking hands is more common. The grip tends to be light and is sustained for a while.

When offering a greeting, you should use a person's family name and appropriate title to address them unless they have said that you can move on to addressing them by using their first name. It's usual for only friends to address one another by using their given names.

Vocabulary builder

01.01 Listen as you look at the words and phrases and repeat what you hear. Then complete the missing English expressions.

nǐ	*you* (sing.)
Nǐ hǎo!	*Hello!* (sing.)
nǐmen	*you* (pl.)
Nǐmen hǎo!	_____
tā	*he/she*
tāmen	_____
xièxie	*thank you; to thank*
xièxie nǐ	_____
xièxie nǐmen	_____
zàijiàn	*goodbye*

When you say *hello* in Chinese to a group of people, which of the two expressions would you use?

a Nǐ hǎo!
b Nǐmen hǎo!

NEW EXPRESSIONS

01.02 Look at the expressions that are used in the dialogues. Note their meanings. Repeat what you hear.

bù	*not*	Nǐ hǎo!	*Hello!* (sing.)
bú yòng xiè	*not at all*	Nǐmen	*you* (pl.)
	(lit. *no need thank*)	Nǐmen hǎo!	*Hello!* (pl.)
bú zài	*not at; not to be at/in*	Qǐng jìn!	*Please come in.*
duìbuqǐ	*excuse me/I'm sorry*	Qǐng wèn, . . . ?	*May I ask . . . ?*
hǎo	*good, well*	Qǐng zuò!	*Please sit down.*
. . . hǎo ma?	*How is/are . . . ?*	tā	*he/she*
hěn	*very*	tàitai	*Mrs; wife*
jīntiān	*today*	xiānsheng	*Mr; husband;*
lái	*to come*		*gentleman*
lǎoshī	*teacher*	xiǎo	*little, small; young*
ma	(question particle)	xièxie	*thank you; to thank*
míngtiān	*tomorrow*	zài	*at; to be at/in*
míngtiān jiàn	*see you tomorrow*	zàijiàn	*goodbye*
nǐ	*you* (sing.)		

1 Nǐ hǎo! Nǐ hǎo ma?   3

Dialogue 1 Saying hello

 01.03 *Mr Wang is a tourist guide. He prefers to be called Xiǎo Wáng (literally little Wang) as he is only 28 years old, although his full name is Wáng Jìjūn. When Mr and Mrs Green see Xiǎo Wáng, they greet him in Chinese.*

1 Listen and follow the text. After the initial greeting, Mrs Green asks Xiǎo Wáng a question. What does that question mean?

Mrs Green	Nǐ hǎo, Xiǎo Wáng!
Mr Green	Xiǎo Wáng, nǐ hǎo!
Xiǎo Wáng	Gélín xiānsheng, Gélín tàitai, nǐmen hǎo!
Mrs Green	Nǐ tàitai hǎo ma?
Xiǎo Wáng	Tā hěn hǎo, xièxie.

 2 Now read the dialogue again and answer the questions.
   a Who is **Gélín xiānsheng**?
   b Who is **Gélín tàitai**?
   c Why does Xiǎo Wáng say **nǐmen hǎo**?
   d How is Xiǎo Wáng's wife?

> **PRONUNCIATION TIP**
> Try saying two 3rd tones together. Difficult, isn't it? Both **nǐ** (*you*) and **hǎo** (*good*) are 3rd tones but when said together **ni** is a 2nd tone. Refer back to the Pronunciation guide for more help.

4

Dialogue 2 Saying goodbye

01.04 *When Mr and Mrs Green have finished their visit, they thank Xiǎo Wáng and say goodbye to him.*

1 **When you thank someone in Chinese, do you say their name first and then *thank you* or the other way round? Listen to the following dialogue and spot which way the speakers say it.**

Mr Green	Xiǎo Wáng, xièxie nǐ.
Mrs Green	Xièxie nǐ, Xiǎo Wáng.
Xiǎo Wáng	Bú yòng xiè.
Mr Green	Zàijiàn.
Xiǎo Wáng	Zàijiàn.
Mrs Green	Zàijiàn.

2 **Now read or listen to the text again and answer the questions.**
   a How would you say *thank you* to more than one person in Chinese?
   b What would you say when someone thanks you?

NEUTRAL TONES

Some syllables or words in Chinese are toneless or have what is called a neutral tone. The **-sheng** of **xiānsheng**, the **-men** in **nǐmen** and the question particle **ma** in the first dialogue are good examples of this.

1 Nǐ hǎo! Nǐ hǎo ma?   5

Dialogue 3 A visitor

01.05 *Mr Green comes to see his Chinese visitor. He knocks at the door.*

1 In the dialogue, you are going to hear two phrases, both of which begin with **Qǐng**. What does each of them mean?

Lǐ	Qǐng jìn.
Mr Green	(enters the room)
Lǐ	Gélín xiānsheng, nǐ hǎo!
Mr Green	Nǐ hǎo, Lǐ xiānsheng.
Lǐ	Qǐng zuò.
Mr Green	Xièxie.
Lǐ	Gélín tàitai hǎo ma?
Mr Green	Tā hěn hǎo. Xièxie.

2 Match the English meaning with the Chinese phrases.

a Qǐng zuò.   1 Please come in.
b Qǐng wèn,   2 May I ask . . . ?
c Qǐng jìn.   3 Please sit down.

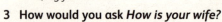

3 How would you ask *How is your wife?*

4 How would you ask *How is your husband?*

Dialogue 4 Visiting a teacher

01.06 *Frank goes to the teachers' office to look for his teacher.*

1 You will hear the expression *See you tomorrow* twice in the dialogue. What is it in Mandarin?

Frank	Qǐng wèn, Zhāng lǎoshī zài ma?
Lǐ lǎoshī	Duìbuqǐ, tā bú zài.
Frank	Tā jīntiān lái ma?
Lǐ lǎoshī	Bù lái. Tā míngtiān lái.
Frank	Xièxie nǐ.
Lǐ lǎoshī	Bú yòng xiè. Míngtiān jiàn.
Frank	Míngtiān jiàn.

2 Did Frank find his teacher in the office?

3 When will Frank be able to see his teacher?

4 Where is Frank's teacher?

5 Look at these sentences from the last conversation. Which underlined word is a question marker? Which underlined word means *well*?
   a Nǐ tàitai <u>hǎo</u> ma?
   b Qǐng wèn, Zhāng lǎoshī zài <u>ma</u>?
   c Xiǎo Wáng, nǐ <u>hǎo</u>!
   d Gélín tàitai hǎo <u>ma</u>?

Language discovery

1 TITLES

In Chinese, the surname or family name always comes first. Traditionally this is the most important thing about your identity. The Chinese have always placed much emphasis on the family. Your title appears after your surname:

Gélín xiānsheng	*Mr Green*
Gélín tàitai	*Mrs Green*
Wáng lǎoshī	*Teacher Wang*

> **LANGUAGE TIP**
> **Nǐ hǎo** can be used at any time to say *Hello* or *How do you do?* You will come across other greetings which refer specifically to the morning or the evening, such as when wishing somebody good night.

1 Nǐ hǎo! Nǐ hǎo ma? 7

2 ASKING SOMEBODY TO DO SOMETHING

Qǐng is used when you want to ask somebody to do something. You use the verb **qǐng** (*to invite/request*) plus the word for whatever you want them to do. Of course **qǐng** could be translated as *please* in such cases.

Qǐng jìn.	*Please come in.*
Qǐng zuò.	*Please sit down.*

You use the verb **wèn** (*to ask*) when you want to ask a question.

wèn wèntí	*to ask (a) question(s)*
Qǐng wèn,	*May I ask . . . ?*

3 'Hǎo' – ADJECTIVE OR VERB?

The answer is both! **Hǎo** is both an adjective (a word that describes a noun) and a verb (a word that tells you what a person, animal or thing does, or is). However, Chinese adjectives can also act as verbs, so **hǎo** means *to be good*, *to be well*, as well as *fine, good, OK*:

Nǐ hǎo.	*How do you do./How are you?*
Tā hěn hǎo.	*He/she is (very) well./ He/she is (very) good.*

But:

hǎo péngyou	*a good friend*
hǎo lǎoshī	*a good teacher*

The use of **hěn** in **hěn hǎo** is not optional. If you do not use it, a comparison is implied. **Hěn** carries a lot less weight than the English *very* unless you stress it.

4 PRONOUNS: YOU LIKE ME? I LIKE YOU!

Pronouns (words used in place of nouns to refer to a person) are very easy in Chinese: **wǒ** means *me* as well as *I*. **Tā** means *him, her, it* as well as *he, she, it*. To make them plural you simply add **-men**. The following table will make this clearer:

wǒ	*I, me*	**wǒmen**	*we, us*
nǐ	*you* (sing.)	**nǐmen**	*you* (pl.)
tā	*he, she, it, him, her*	**tāmen**	*they, them*

Although *he*, *she* and *it* are all pronounced **tā**, each of them is written with a different character. This only affects the written language, so there is absolutely nothing to worry about.

5 SIMPLE QUESTIONS WITH 'MA'?

To make a question from any statement you just put **ma** at the end of it.

Tā míngtiān lái.	*She is coming tomorrow.*
Tā míngtiān lái ma?	*Is she coming tomorrow?*
Wáng lǎoshī zài.	*Teacher Wang is around.*
Wáng lǎoshī zài ma?	*Is Teacher Wang around?*

6 HOW TO SAY NO!

To make a verb negative in Chinese all you have to do is put **bù** in front of it. There is only one exception to this rule, which you will meet in Unit 2.

Nǐ hǎo.	*You're well/good.*
Nǐ bù hǎo.	*You're not well/not good.*
Tā zài.	*He/she's here.*
Tā bú zài.	*He/she's not here.*

7 WORD ORDER THAT'S DIFFERENT BUT NOT DIFFICULT!

Basic Chinese word order is the same as in English:

I   like   you
subject   verb   object

but in English, you say *He is coming tomorrow*, whereas in Chinese, you say:

Tā míngtiān lái.   *He tomorrow comes.*

To sum up, time words like *today, tomorrow, Wednesday, 6 o'clock* come before the verb in Chinese. Other words that come before the verb are the negative **bù**, and words such as **yě** (*also*) and **hěn** (*very*).

8 PLEASE AND THANK YOU

Qǐng (*please*) and **xièxie** (*thank you*) are used much less frequently in Chinese than in English, but it is always better to use them too much rather than too little!

Practice

1 **Now let's practise some language points you have learned in this unit.**
   a How do you address a married couple?
   b Say the word *good*.
   c Then ask the question *Is it good?*
   d Say the singular pronouns for *I*, *you*, *he* and *she*.
   e Then say the plural form of these pronouns.

2 **What do you say? Choose the most appropriate response and say it out loud.**
   a When you greet a friend, you say:
      Nǐ hǎo   Zàijiàn   Bú yòng xiè   Xièxie
   b When you thank someone, you say:
      Zàijiàn   Nǐ hǎo   Xièxie   Bú yòng xiè
   c When someone thanks you for your help, you respond by saying:
      Nǐ hǎo   Bú yòng xiè   Zàijiàn   Xièxie

3 **Respond to a Chinese person. To help you out, the first letter of the correct response is already put in.**

   Example: Qǐng jìn. – Xièxie.

   a Nǐ hǎo!   N_____!
   b Xièxie nǐ.   B_____.
   c Qǐng zuò.   X_____.
   d Zàijiàn!   Z_____!

4 **This time you begin and the Chinese person responds. Now you're on your own.**
   a _____.   Nǐ hǎo!
   b Lǐ tàitai _____?   Ta hěn hǎo. Xièxie nǐ.
   c Lǐ xiānsheng _____?   Duìbuqǐ, tā bú zài.
   d _____.   Bú yòng xiè.

5 What would you put in each of the gaps to turn them into words or phrases?

Example: Duì_____ qǐ. – Duìbuqǐ.

a Xiè _____.
b _____ xiè.
c _____ jiàn!
d _____ jiàn!
e Qǐng _____.
f _____ zuò.
g _____ hǎo.
h _____ hǎo _____ ?

6 Match the sentences on the left to those on the right.

a Tāmen hěn hǎo.   1 They won't be in tomorrow.
b Tāmen jīntiān bú zài.   2 They will come today.
c Tāmen jīntiān lái.   3 They are not in today.
d Tāmen míngtiān bú zài.   4 They are very well.

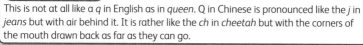

HOW TO PRONOUNCE 'Q'

This is not at all like a *q* in English as in *queen*. Q in Chinese is pronounced like the *j* in *jeans* but with air behind it. It is rather like the *ch* in *cheetah* but with the corners of the mouth drawn back as far as they can go.

7 01.07 Now listen to the following sounds/syllables and identify which ones contain the sound *q*.

a jing
b qing
c xing
d qin
e qi

1 Nǐ hǎo! Nǐ hǎo ma?

Test yourself

1 **01.08 What would you say in the following situations?**
   a You meet your Chinese friend, Mr Li, and you want to say *hello*.
   b Then you ask how his wife is.
   c You are a little bit late and you say you are sorry.
   d Thank your friend (for their help).
   e When they thank you, say *You're welcome*.
   f When you take your leave, what do you say?

2 **Vocabulary and pronunciation**
   a Is the tone for *you* in Chinese 1st, 2nd, 3rd or 4th tone?
   b Is the Chinese for *teacher* **lǎoshī** or **xiānsheng**?
   c Which word means *tomorrow*? Is it **míngtiān** or **jīntiān**?
   d Which syllable in **míngtiān jiàn** and **zàijiàn** means *to see*?

SELF CHECK

I CAN...
...greet people.
...address people formally
...thank people.
...say goodbye.
...tell the difference between single and plural in common pronouns.
...ask whether someone is available/present.

Below you can see two 'signs' or 'drawings'. Each of these is known as a Chinese 'character'. Chinese writing is not phonetic. This means that you cannot learn to 'read' Chinese characters in the same way as you can learn to read English but have to learn each character separately. You'll learn more about this as we go along.

You will notice that the characters do not have any resemblance to the pinyin, the sound representation of the characters which is **rùkǒu**. The first character means *enter* but this would be very hard to guess. What does the second character look like?

Rùkǒu
Entrance

KEY CHARACTERS

欢迎 Huānyíng
Welcome

再见 Zàijiàn
Goodbye

2

In this unit you will learn how to:
» say who you are.
» make simple introductions.
» ask who other people are.
» address people correctly.
» deny something.

Nǐ jiào shénme?

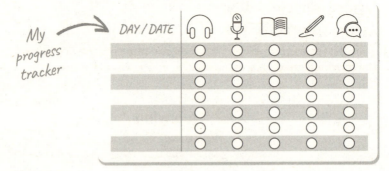

Names

02.01 There are far fewer surnames in Chinese than in English. You are going to hear quite a few of them in this unit. You will now hear 10 of the most common Chinese surnames. Listen and repeat each one after the speaker.

Zhāng Wáng Lǐ Zhào Liú
张 王 李 赵 刘

Chén Lín Wú Guō Zhèng
陈 林 吴 郭 郑

HOW TO BE COURTEOUS

The use of first names is generally reserved for family members and close friends. Colleagues or people in your peer group are addressed on an informal basis by their surnames prefaced by **lǎo** (*old*) or **xiǎo** (*young*), largely depending on whether the person in question is older or younger than you. When you don't know somebody very well (or at all) or you wish to show respect (usually for older people, teachers, etc.), you use **nín** instead of **nǐ**. It is, however, used less frequently than it used to be and it cannot be used in the plural. This means that the plural form of both nǐ and nín is nǐmen, nǐmen being both heard and read frequently in daily life.

Which would you use in the following situations?

1 You address your Chinese partner's mother or father in person. Which of the following do you use?
   a nǐ b nín

2 What do you use when addressing both of them together?
   a nǐmen b nín

3 When you check into a hotel and speak to the receptionist which do you use?
   a nǐ b nín

Vocabulary builder

ASKING SOMEONE'S NAME

02.02 Listen as you look at the words and phrases. Then complete the missing English expressions.

guì	expensive, honourable
xìng	surname
Nín guì xìng?	What's your (honourable) name?
jiào	to call/be called
míngzi	name
shénme?	what?
Nǐ jiào shénme míngzi?	_____
shéi/shuí?	who?
shì	to be
Nǐ shì shéi?	_____
Tā shì shéi?	_____

1 What are the two ways of asking someone what their name is?

2 When you want to ask someone who they are, what do you ask?
   a Tā shì shéi? b Nǐ shì shéi?

NEW EXPRESSIONS

02.03 Look at the words and phrases used in the following dialogue. Note their meanings and repeat what you hear.

háizi	child/children
méi	no, not (have not)
nà/nèi (used interchangeably)	that
nín	you (polite form)
wǒ	I; me
yǒu	to have

2 Nǐ jiào shénme?

zhè/zhèi (used interchangeably)	this
Nǐ/tā jiào shénme (míngzi)?	What is your/his/her name?
Wǒ/tā jiào . . .	I am/he is/she is called . . .
Zhè/nà (bú) shì . . .	This/that is (not) . . .

Dialogue 1 Asking each other's name

 1 02.04 Listen and follow the dialogue. Who is Pàn Pan? Is he Ms Lord's child or Mrs Li's child?

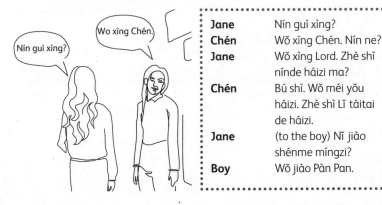

Jane	Nín guì xìng?
Chén	Wǒ xìng Chén. Nín ne?
Jane	Wǒ xìng Lord. Zhè shì nínde háizi ma?
Chén	Bú shì. Wǒ méi yǒu háizi. Zhè shì Lǐ tàitai de háizi.
Jane	(to the boy) Nǐ jiào shénme míngzi?
Boy	Wǒ jiào Pàn Pan.

 2 Now read or listen to the dialogue again and answer these questions.

   a How many people are there in the dialogue?
   b What are the family names/surnames of the women?
   c Does Ms Chen have children?

> **TIP**
> While personal questions such as whether you have children may be considered impolite in the West, they are very common in China, as you will learn in the next unit.

NEW EXPRESSIONS

02.05 **Look at the words and phrases used in the following dialogue. Note their meanings and repeat what you hear.**

dāngrán	of course
huì	can, to be able to
méi guānxi	it's OK, it doesn't matter
shuō	to speak, to say
yě	also
yìdiǎn(r)	a little

Yīngwén	*English (language)*
Zhōngwén	*Chinese (language)*

Dialogue 2 At a conference

02.06 *Two participants at a conference get to know each other a little better.*

1 **In Chinese do you say the surname first and then the title (Mr, Mrs) or do you say the title first and then the surname as in English? Listen to the following dialogue and spot which way the speakers say it.**

White	Zhèng xiānsheng, nǐ hǎo!
Cháng	Wǒ xìng Cháng, bú xìng Zhèng. Wǒ jiào Cháng Zhèng.
White	Duìbuqǐ, Cháng xiānsheng.
Cháng	Méi guānxi. White xiānsheng, nǐ yǒu mei yǒu Zhōngwén míngzi?
White	Yǒu. Wǒ jiào Bái Bǐdé.
Cháng	Bái xiānsheng, nǐ huì bu huì shuō Yīngwén?
White	Dāngrán huì. Cháng xiānsheng, nǐ yě huì shuō Yīngwén ma?
Cháng	Huì yìdiǎnr.

2 **What is the Chinese man's surname?**
   a Chang
   b Zheng

3 **How good is the Chinese man's English?**
   a He speaks well.
   b He speaks a little.

> **TONE OF 'BÙ'**
>
> **Bù** (*not*) is normally a 4th tone, but it becomes a 2nd tone before another 4th tone. When this happens it is marked as such in the text, such as **bú xìng** not **bù xìng**. It is toneless in such expressions as **huì bu huì** (see Dialogue 2).

2 Nǐ jiào shénme? 17

NEW EXPRESSIONS

02.07 Look at the words and phrases used in the following dialogues. Note their meanings and repeat what you hear.

nán	*male*	xiǎojie	*Miss*
Nǐ ne?	*And you?*	zhēn	*real; really*
niánqīng	*young*	wǒ shì	*I am*
péngyou	*friend*	wǒ bú shì	*I am not*
piàoliang	*good-looking*	nǐ shì	*you are*
rènshi	*to recognize;*	nǐ bú shì	*you are not*
	to know (people)	tā shì	*he/she is*
shéi/shuí?	*who?*	tā bú shì	*he/she is not*
wǒde	*my*	Tā shì shéi?	*Who is he or she?*
nǐde	*your*	Tā shì bu shì . . . ?	*Is he or she . . . (or not)*
nínde	*your (polite)*		
tāde	*his/her*		

Dialogue 3 Meeting people

1 **02.08** How does the person in the following dialogue introduce himself?

a Wǒ shì Bái Bǐdé. b Wǒ jiào Bái Bǐdé.

Bái	Nà shì shéi? Nǐ rènshi bu rènshi tā?
Wú	Rènshi. Tā shì Guō xiǎojie.
Bái	Tā zhēn piàoliang.
	(walks over to the girl)
Bái	Nǐ hǎo! Wǒ jiào Bái Bǐdé. Nǐ ne?
Guō	Nǐ hǎo! Wǒ jiào Guō Yùjié.
	(A man walks over to her and hands her a drink.)
Guō	Zhè shì wǒde nán péngyou. Tā jiào Liú Wénguāng. Zhè shì Bái xiānsheng.
Liú	Bái xiānsheng, nǐ hǎo!
Bái	O, nǐ hǎo!

2 How would you say she is good-looking?

a Nǐ zhēn piàoliang. b Tā zhēn piàoliang.

3 How would you introduce your friend to another person?

a Zhè shì wǒde péngyou. b Wǒ shì tāde péngyou.

4 How would you ask someone whether they know another person?

   a Nǐ rènshi bu rènshi tā?   **b** Tā rènshi bu rènshi nǐ?

Practice 1

Read the dialogues again to find the appropriate words to complete the sentences.

1 Nín guì _____?
2 Nǐ huì bu _____ shuō Yīngwén?
3 Tā _____ Liú Wénguāng
4 Wǒ _____ yǒu háizi.

Language discovery

1 PRONOUNS AND POSSESSIVES: YOU AND YOURS

Nǐ means *you* (sing.). If you add the little word **de** to it, it means *your* or *yours*:

nǐde háizi	*your child*
wǒde xiānsheng	*my husband*
zhè shì nǐde	*this is yours*
Lǐ tàitai de háizi	*Mrs Li's child*
tāde háizi	*his/her child*

In close personal relationships: **nǐ tàitai** (*your wife*), **wǒ māma** (*my mum*), the **de** may be omitted (see Unit 1, Dialogue 1, where Mrs Green asks Xiǎo Wáng, **Nǐ tàitai hǎo ma?**).

Whereas **de** may be omitted in **nǐ tàitai** and **wǒ māma**, it may not be omitted in **Lǐ tàitai de háizi**. How do you remember when you can or can't omit **de**? The simplest way to remember this is that **de** may be omitted when single syllable pronouns (**wǒ**, **nǐ** and **tā**) are used.

2 NEGATIVES: HOW TO SAY NO WITH 'YǑU'

To say *do not have* in Chinese, you put **méi** in front of the verb **yǒu** *to have*. For present or future actions all other verbs are negated by putting **bù** in front of them.

Wǒ méi yǒu háizi.	*I have no children.*
Tā méi yǒu Zhōngwén míngzi.	*She doesn't have a Chinese name.*

2 Nǐ jiào shénme?

1 **Yǒu** in **méi yǒu** is sometimes omitted in colloquial speech. So you may say **Wǒ méi yǒu háizi** or **Wǒ méi háizi**. Now answer these questions in Chinese.
   a Nǐ yǒu háizi ma?
   b Nǐ yǒu péngyou ma?
   c Nǐ yǒu Zhōngwén míngzi ma?

3 ANOTHER WAY OF ASKING QUESTIONS

If you put the positive and negative forms of the verb together (in that order) you can make a question:

Nǐ yǒu mei yǒu háizi?	*Do you have children?*
Nǐ shì bu shì lǎoshī?	*Are you a teacher?*

This is a popular alternative to the question form with **ma** (see Language discovery 5 in Unit 1). The negative form of the verb is normally unstressed when it is used to make a question in this way. It is stressed, however, if the question is said slowly or with emphasis.

2 **Turn the following questions into the choice type of question.**
   a Nǐ yǒu háizi ma? ⟶ Nǐ yǒu mei yǒu háizi?
   b Nǐ rènshi tā ma?   _____
   c Tā hǎo ma?   _____
   d Nǐmen shuō Zhōngwén ma? _____

4 YES AND NO IN REPLIES

Yes and *no* don't exist as such in Chinese. If you are asked a question the answer is either the positive form of the verb (to mean *yes*) or the negative form of the verb (to mean *no*):

Nǐ yǒu méi yǒu háizi?	*Do you have children?*
Yǒu.	*Yes, I do.*
Méi yǒu.	*No, I don't.*
Nǐ rènshi tā ma?	*Do you know her?*
Rènshi.	*Yes, I do.*
Bú rènshi.	*No, I don't.*

5 TO BE OR NOT TO BE?

Shì, the verb *to be* in English, is used much less in Chinese than in English. This is because adjectives in Chinese can also act as verbs, as you saw in Unit 1. For example, **hǎo** means *to be good* as well as *good* so there is no need for the verb *to be*.

Zhè shì nǐde háizi ma?	*Is this your child?*
Bú shì. Zhè shì Lǐ tàitai de háizi.	*No, it's Mrs Li's child.*
Tā shì nǐde nǚ péngyou ma?	*Is she your girlfriend?*
Bú shì. Tā shì wǒ tàitai.	*No, she's my wife.*

6 QUESTION WORDS: WHO? AND WHAT?

In Chinese, question words such as **shéi** (*who*) and **shénme** (*what*) appear in the sentence in the same position as the word or words which replace them in the answer:

Nǐ jiào shénme míngzi?	*What are you called?* (lit. *You are called what?*)
Wǒ jiào Pàn Pan.	*I'm called Pàn Pan.*
Nà shì shéi?	*Who is that (young woman)?* (lit. *That (young woman) is who?*)
Tā shì wǒ (de) péngyou.	*She is my friend.*

This is different from the word order in English, where the question word is at the beginning of the sentence.

3 Ask these questions in Chinese. Pay attention to the position of the question word.

a What's his name?
b Who do you know?
c What do they have?

7 FOLLOW-UP QUESTIONS

To avoid having to ask a question in full or to repeat the same question you can use the little word **ne** at the end of a phrase to take a short cut!

Nǐ jiào shénme míngzi?	*What's your name?*
Wǒ jiào Wú Zébì. Nǐ ne?	*I'm called/My name is Wú Zébì. What about you?* (i.e. *what's your name?*)
Wǒ jiào Mǎ Tiān. Tā ne?	*My name's Tim Marr. What's hers?*

As you have seen in both Units 1 and 2, the surname or family name comes before your title in Chinese. This means that your given name (first name) comes after your surname:

Cháng (family name) **Zhèng** (given name)

Bái (family name) **Bǐdé** (given name)

2 Nǐ jiào shénme? 21

Practice 2

1 **Complete the following exchanges by filling in the blanks in the sentences:**
   a Tā jiào _____ míngzi? Tā _____ Fāng Yuán.
   b Nǐ _____ shuō Zhōngwén ma? Huì. Wǒ huì _____ yìdiǎnr.
   c Tāde nán péngyou _____ shéi? Wǒ bú _____ tā.

2 **Look at the pictures and answer the following questions in Chinese:**

   a Tāmen shì shéi?
   ← b Tā jiào shénme?
   c Tā xìng Yīng ma? →
   ← d Tā yě xìng Yīng ma?
   e Nǐ rènshi tāmen ma?

Lǐ Jīnshēng   **Yīng Zìpéng**

3 02.09 **Answer the questions about the woman in the following listening passage.**

Wǒde Zhōngwén lǎoshī jiào Wáng Lányīng. Tā hěn niánqīng. Tā yǒu hěn duō péngyou. Tāmen bú rènshi nǐ. Tāmen huì shuō yìdiǎnr Yīngwén.
   a What's her surname?
   b What's her first name?
   c How much English does she speak?
   d What is her occupation?
   e Does she know you?
   f What age is she?
   g Does she have a lot of friends?

4 Who is who? State the name and the occupation of each person pictured. You will get more practice if you use both of the patterns given in the following example:

Example: Tā jiào Yán Lóng. Tā shì xuésheng (*student*).
Zhè/nà shì Yán Lóng. Tā shì xuésheng.

a Zhào Huá	b Liú Guāng	c Guā Jié
jǐngchá	sījī	yīshēng
d Lǐ Mínglì	e Zhōu Jiābǎo	f Wú Zébì
lǎoshī	xuésheng	chúshī

5 According to the pictures in the previous question, are the following statements true or false? If true, say duì, which means correct. If it's not true, say bú duì, which means not correct.

Example: Zhào Huá xìng Huá.   bú duì
a Zhào Huá shì lǎoshī.   **d** Zhōu Jiābǎo xìng Jiābǎo.
b Liú Guāng bú shì sījī.   **e** Lǐ lǎoshī jiào Lǐ Míng.
c Nà ge yīshēng jiào Wú Zébì.   **f** Wú Zébì shì chúshī.

6 You have learnt two ways to ask questions. With each set of words use these different question forms to make up two questions. The example will make this clear.

Example: Tā/huì shuō/Fǎwén (*French*)
– Tā huì shuō Fǎwén ma?
– Tā huì bú huì shuō Fǎwén?

a Nǐ/huì shuō/Yīngwén   **d** Lǐ xiānsheng/jīntiān/lái
b Nǐmen/shì/lǎoshī   **e** Wáng Fāng/yǒu/Yīngwén míngzi
c Xiǎo Zhèng/zài   **f** Lín lǎoshī/jiào/Lín Péng

2 Nǐ jiào shénme?

Test yourself

1 02.10 **Now you've arrived at the end of Unit 2. How would you say the following?**
   a Ask what a person's surname is.
   b Say *My name is X*.
   c Say that you haven't got a Chinese name.
   d Say that you don't know her.
   e Say *That's OK* when someone apologizes to you.
   f Say that your friend is not a teacher.

2 **Vocabulary and pronunciation**
   a Is the pronunciation for *of course* **dānrán** or **dāngrán**?
   b What is the Chinese for *to speak/to say*? Is it **shuō** or **shōu**?
   c The Chinese for *who* can be pronounced in two ways: **shuí** or_____?
   d The Chinese for *English (language)* and *Chinese (language)* is **Yīngwén** and **Zhōngwén** respectively. What syllable in these two words means *language*?

SELF CHECK

I CAN...
...introduce myself.
...introduce another person to others.
...ask who someone is.
...ask someone's name in a polite way.
...deny something is so by saying *he/she/it is not* or *I/you/he/she doesn't have*, etc.

# KEY CHARACTERS

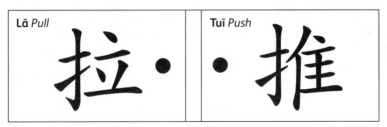

Lā *Pull*

Tuī *Push*

The left-hand side of these two characters is the same. That is because both the actions of pulling and pushing require a hand to do it with. The left-hand side represents a hand in each case. This is the meaning part of the character. It does not always occur on the left-hand side of a character.

On its own the hand is pronounced **shǒu**.

3

In this unit you will learn how to:
» say where you come from and what nationality you are.
» ask for and give an address.
» say the numbers 0–10.
» ask for, and give, a phone number.
» fill out a form.

Nǐ shì nǎ guó rén?

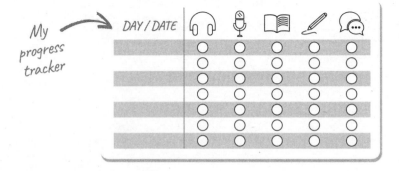

Questions

Chinese people are very direct with their questions. It is not considered rude to ask how old you are, how much you earn, how much your house cost to buy and so on.

Even questions about your shape and size or why you haven't married or why you got divorced are all considered perfectly legitimate.

Talking about where you come from, what nationality you are, where you live and your phone number is straightforward in Chinese with the necessary vocabulary and a few of the basic rules about word order. Chinese numbers are very easy as you will discover in this unit. In this unit keep practising how to ask other people where they come from (**Nín shì nǎ guó rén?**), where they live (**Nǐ zhù zài nǎr?**) and what their phone number is (**Nǐde diànhuà hàomǎ shì duōshao?**). Make sure you can answer these questions yourself! Aim at answering them without thinking.

You are at an international business meeting where you know hardly anyone.

1 How do you introduce yourself and how do you ask somebody their name? (You might need to refer back to Unit 2 to refresh your memory.)
2 You arrange to meet one of the participants later that day. How do you ask them for their phone number so that you can make the arrangements?

Vocabulary builder

03.01 **Listen as you look at the words and phrases and repeat what you hear.**

ba	question tag indicating suggestion
duì	yes, correct
Guǎngdōng	Canton (Province)
guó	country
Lúndūn	London
míngpiàn	name card
nǎ	which?
nǎr?	where?
rén	person
Yīngguó	England (Britain)
Zhōngguó	China
zhù	to live
zhù zài	to live in/at a place

1 The meaning of **rén** is *person*. What is the meaning of **Lúndūn-rén**?
2 What is the meaning of **Yīngguó-rén**?
3 What is the meaning of **Zhōngguó-rén**?

NEW EXPRESSIONS

03.02 **These expressions are used in the following dialogues. Note their meanings and repeat what you hear.**

fàndiàn	hotel
fēijī	plane
hépíng	peace
piào	ticket
xǐhuan	to like
yìsi	meaning

3 Nǐ shì nǎ guó rén?

Dialogue 1 Where are you from?

 03.03 *Mr Peter White (Bái Bǐdé) meets a Chinese person, Lín Jiànmù, at a conference.*

1 What would you say when handing out your name card to another person?

Lín	Nín shì nǎ guó rén?
Bái	Wǒ shì Yīngguó-rén. Zhè shì wǒde míngpiàn.
Lín	Xièxie. O, Bái xiānsheng, nín zhù zài Lúndūn?
Bái	Duì. Nín shì Zhōngguó-rén ba?
Lín	Shì, wǒ shì Guǎngdōng-rén.

2 You heard Mr White say **Nín shì Zhōngguó-rén ba?** What does it mean?

3 What's the difference in meaning between this question and **Nín shì Zhōngguó-rén ma?**

> **TIP**
> Chinese business people don't hand out business cards any more. They all scan each other's WeChat code. However, visitors who don't use WeChat may still need to prepare and present name cards.

Dialogue 2 At passport control

 03.04 *Bái xiānsheng is at passport control at Beijing Capital Airport.*

1 What is the name of the hotel that Mr White will be staying at?

Officer	Qǐng gěi wǒ kànkan nín de fēijī piào.
Bái	Zhè shì wǒ de fēijī piào.
Officer	Nǐ zhù zài shénme fàndiàn?
Bái	Hépíng fàndiàn
Officer	Hépíng fàndiàn?
Bái	Duì. Hépíng shì *peace* de yìsi. Wǒ xǐhuān hépíng.
Officer	Xièxiè nín.

2 What does the name of the hotel mean in English?

3 You have learnt the words **fēijī** and **piào**. What is a **fēijī piào**?

4 What is the meaning of **yìsi**?

28

NUMBERS 0–10

03.05

0	1	2	3	4	5	6	7	8	9	10
líng	yī	èr	sān	sì	wǔ	liù	qī	bā	jiǔ	shí
〇/零*	一	二	三	四	五	六	七	八	九	十

* Nowadays Chinese people often use 〇 instead of the Chinese character 零 which is quite complicated to write.

1 Practise saying 1 to 5: **yī èr sān sì wǔ**. Then say 6 to 10: **liù qī bā jiǔ shí**. Then try both sets together.

2 Now say **yī sān wǔ qī jiǔ**. Then say **èr sì liù bā shí**.

3 Now try this: **yī èr sān, sān èr yī, yī èr sān sì wǔ liù qī**.

MORE NEW EXPRESSIONS

03.06 **Look at the expressions that are used in the following dialogue. Note their meanings. Repeat what you hear.**

diànhuà	phone (lit. electric speech)
Dōngchéng (Qū)	Eastern City (District)
duōshao?	what's the number of?
fàndiàn	hotel
fángjiān	room
hào	number
hàomǎ	number (often used for phones and car registration plates)
jǐ hào?	which number?
lù	road, street
nǎr?	where?
piào	ticket
píng'ān	safe and sound
qū	district
Xīchéng (Qū)	Western City (District)

3 Nǐ shì nǎ guó rén?

Dialogue 3 Phone numbers

 03.07 *Mr White and Mr Lin share their contact details.*

1 What is the room number?

Lín	Nǐ zhù zài nǎr?
Bái	Wǒ zhù zài Hépíng Fàndiàn.
Lín	Jǐ hào fángjiān?
Bái	Wǔ-líng-bā hào fángjiān. Nǐ zhù zài nǎr?
Lín	Wǒ zhù zài Píng'ān Lù qī hào.
Bái	Píng'ān Lù zài nǎr?
Lín	Píng'ān Lù zài Xīchéng Qū.
Bái	Hépíng Fàndiàn yě zài Xīchéng Qū shì bu shi?
Lín	Bú zài. Zài Dōngchéng Qū.
Bái	Nǐde gōngsī de diànhuà hàomǎ shì duōshao?
Lín	Liù-wǔ-wǔ-èr jiǔ-sān-èr-sì. Nǐde ne?
Bái	Wǒde gōngsī de shì liù-liù-qī-sān bā-bā-sān-líng.

2 You have heard four phrases related to places in the conversation. Would you be able to construct two sentences to show how they are related by using the pattern: A **zài** *place word*? The four phrases are: **Hépíng Fàndiàn, Píng'ān Lù, Xīchéng Qū** and **Dōngchéng Qū**.

3 Do you remember **Xīchéng (Qū)** and **Dōngchéng (Qū)**? Clearly, **xī** and **dōng** at the beginning of the words mean two opposite directions. Do they mean *east and west* or *west and east* respectively?

4 You have learned **hǎo** and **hào**. They are different only in tone. What do they mean respectively?

 5 Listen to the conversation again and see if you can write down Mr Lin's and Mr White's phone numbers. You might have to listen to it at least twice to get them both down correctly.

Language discovery

1 WHERE ARE YOU FROM?

To give your nationality you say the name of the country and then add **-rén** *person* after it:

Zhōngguó	*China, Chinese*
Zhōngguó-rén	*Chinese person*
Měiguó	*USA*
Měiguó-rén	*American*

> **PRONUNCIATION TIP**
>
> Foreign names, such as the names of countries and cities, can be expressed in Chinese in three main ways:
> Based on the original sound, such as **Yìdàlì** (*Italy*).
> Based on the meaning, such as **Niújīn** (*Oxford*) (lit. *ox/cow ford*).
> A mixture of the original sound and its meaning, such as **Xīn** (*New*) **Xīlán** (*Zealand*).
>
> 1 Try pronouncing the names of the countries on the maps that follow. Repeat them out loud over and over again.
> 2 Every time you stumble over the pronunciation of a word or syllable go back to the Pronunciation guide and check it out.

Look at the two maps and the table between them to see exactly how this works.

COUNTRIES AND NATIONALITIES

03.08

Country	Nationality	Country/Nationality
Ài'ěrlán	Ài'ěrlán-rén	*Ireland/Irish*
Àodàlìyà	Àodàlìyà-rén	*Australia/Australian*
Bāxī	Bāxī-rén	*Brazil/Brazilian*
Déguó	Déguó-rén	*Germany/German*
Fǎguó	Fǎguó-rén	*France/French*
Kěnníyà	Kěnníyà-rén	*Kenya/Kenyan*
Měiguó	Měiguó-rén	*USA/American*
Mòxīgē	Mòxīgē-rén	*Mexico/Mexican*
Nírìlìyà	Nírìlìyà-rén	*Nigeria/Nigerian*
Rìběn	Rìběn-rén	*Japan/Japanese*
Yīngguó	Yīngguó-rén	*Britain/British (often also used for England/English)*
Yuènán	Yuènán-rén	*Vietnam/Vietnamese*
Xiānggǎng	Xiānggǎng-rén	*Hong Kong/from Hong Kong*
Xīnjiāpō	Xīnjiāpō-rén	*Singapore/Singaporean*
Zhōngguó	Zhōngguó-rén	*China/Chinese*

FOREIGN NAMES

When translating a foreign name, either a place name or a person's name, the Chinese usually try to find characters that sound similar to the foreign pronunciation. From the list already given, you can see that most of them sound close to their English pronunciation. However, as there are many homophones or characters that sound similar to each other, it can be a delicate matter as to which characters to choose. There are, of course, nicer words and less desirable words which sound similar. Although each character has its own meaning, they would usually not make sense if they were translated back into English. For example, the three characters for **Ài'ěrlán**, which sounds close to *Ireland*, mean *love*, *thou* (classical) and *cymbidium*. You would probably need to stretch your imagination a little further to come up with a meaningful explanation. However, for some names, you would probably accept them as more than just acceptable. Here are some examples:

Měiguó	*beautiful country*
Yīngguó	*heroic country*
Déguó	*virtuous country*

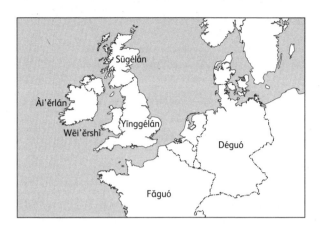

You do exactly the same thing when you wish to say which province or town you come from:

Wǒ shì Lúndūn-rén.	*I'm a Londoner.*
Nǐ shì Luómǎ-rén ma?	*Are you from Rome?*
Tā shì bu shì Běijīng-rén?	*Is he from Beijing?*
Wǒmen shì Fújiàn-rén.	*We're from Fujian Province.*
Tāmen shì Guǎngdōng-rén.	*They're from Guangdong Province.*

2 QUESTION TAG 'BA'

Ba is placed after a verb or phrase to make a suggestion or to ask for confirmation of a supposition:

Nǐ shì Zhōngguó-rén ba?	*You're Chinese, I take it?*
Hǎo ba?	*Is that all right then?*

3 LINKING WORD 'DE'

You have to reverse the word order in Chinese to translate a phrase such as *the meaning of hépíng*. The two words **hépíng** (*peace*) and **yìsi** (*meaning*) are linked by the little word **de**.

hépíng de yìsi	*the meaning of hépíng*

Some people call this the possessive **de** to distinguish it from another **de** you will meet in Unit 8.

Look carefully at the following examples:

'Fàndiàn' de yìsi shì 'hotel'.	*The meaning of 'fàndiàn' is 'hotel'.*
Bái xiānsheng de diànhuà hàomǎ	*Mr White's phone number*
Mǎ tàitai de háizi	*Mrs Ma's child*

3 Nǐ shì nǎ guó rén?

4 ROOM 508

Room 508 is said as *508 room* in Chinese (the reverse of English word order) with the addition of the word **hào** (*number*) after 508. Here are some more examples:

10 (shí) hào	number 10
5 (wǔ) hào fángjiān	room 5

Room numbers up to 100 are generally said as one number. You will meet numbers from 10 to 100 in the next unit.

Numbers over 100 are broken down into single digits:

374 (sān-qī-sì) hào fángjiān	room 374
896 (bā-jiǔ-liù) hào fángjiān	room 896

5 QUESTION TAG 'SHÌ BU SHI?'

Making a question by putting **shì bu shi?** at the end of a sentence in Chinese conveys the idea of *Am I right?* or *Is it true?*:

Hépíng Fàndiàn yě zài Xīchéng Qū shì bu shi?	*The Peace Hotel is also in the Western City District, isn't it?*
Nǐ shì Yīngguó-rén shì bu shi?	*You're English/British, aren't you?*

PHONE NUMBERS

In major cities, landline numbers consist of a two-digit area code followed by an eight-digit local number. In other places, landline numbers consist of a three-digit area code followed by a seven- or eight-digit local number. Mobile phone numbers consist of eleven digits.

8 **bā** is considered to be a lucky number in China and people are prepared to pay for certain numbers containing more 8s in their phone numbers.

To remind yourself again, here are the numbers 1-9, followed by zero:

yī èr sān sì wǔ liù qī bā jiǔ líng

Yāo is used instead of **yī** when phone numbers or large numbers for rooms, buses, trains, and so on are broken down into single digits. This avoids any confusion with **qī** (*seven*). Here are the numbers 1-9 (followed by zero) again, but using **yāo** instead of **yī**:

yāo èr sān sì wǔ liù qī bā jiǔ líng

Here are some eight-digit numbers for you to practise saying out loud:

5188 6188	**wǔ yāo bā bā liù yāo bā bā**
1357 2468	**yāo sān wǔ qī èr sì liù bā**

| 1234 2345 | yāo èr sān sì èr sān sì wǔ |
| 3456 4567 | sān sì wǔ liù sì wǔ liù qī |

Mobile numbers usually start with 13, 15 and 18. Here are three for you to practise saying out loud:

130 2468 6789	yāo sān líng èr sì liù bā liù qī bā jiǔ
150 3456 4567	yāo wǔ líng sān sì wǔ liù sì wǔ liù qī
180 1234 2345	yāo bā líng yāo èr sān sì èr sān sì wǔ

These days when people ask for your phone number, (practise repeating **Nǐde diànhuà shì duōshǎo?**), they are invariably asking for your mobile number. If they wish to have your landline number, they would specifically say so.

Practice

1 Have imaginary conversations with yourself in Chinese using the material in the dialogues and the structures you have covered. For example, a Chinese person may ask where you live. Or you may ask a Chinese person where they are staying. Here are some English examples as a guide.

A Where do you live?
B I live at No. 10 Downing Street.

A Where are you staying?
B Peace Hotel. Room 305.

2 Think of somebody and say everything you can about them in Chinese: what their name is, what nationality they are, where they live, what their phone number is, whether they have children, if you like them, and so on. Then do the same thing with somebody else, and so on, until you can go through the whole routine without hesitation.

DON'T WORRY ABOUT MAKING MISTAKES!

Anybody who has successfully learnt a foreign language knows that the way to make progress is to listen and speak as much as possible. Don't worry if you don't understand a lot of what is said to you in the beginning – just respond to what you do understand.

You will find the following two sentences very useful. Practise them over and over again:

3 Nǐ shì nǎ guó rén?

Qǐng nǐ shuō màn yìdiǎn.   *Please speak more slowly.* (lit. invite you say slow a little)

Qǐng nǐ zài shuō yí biàn.   *Please say it again.* (lit. invite you again say one time)

This **zài** is not the **zài** which means *to be in/at*; it is the **zài** which means *again* as in **zàijiàn** (*goodbye*) (lit. *again see*). Words like **zài** (*again*) are called adverbs. They come before the verb in Chinese.

3 **Answer the following questions. If you don't know, say Wǒ bù zhīdao** (lit. *I not know*):
  a Nǐ shì Měiguó-rén ma?
  b Nǐ māma (*mum*) shì Fǎguó-rén ma?
  c Nǐde lǎoshī shì Zhōngguó-rén ba?
  d Nǐ bàba (*dad*) bú shì Déguó-rén ba?
  e Xí Jìnpíng shì Zhōngguó-rén ma?
  f Shāshìbǐyà (*Shakespeare*) shì bu shì Yīngguó-rén?

4 03.09 **You are going to hear three people introducing themselves. Listen twice and take notes while you are doing so. Then fill in as many details about each of the three speakers as you can. Listen again, paying particular attention to the bits you have not been able to catch. Listen for a fourth time to check what you have written.**

	Speaker 1	Speaker 2	Speaker 3
Surname			
Given name			
Nationality			
Phone no			
Address			
– city			
– street			
– number			

If you're still not sure of what you've heard, have a look at what the three people say in the Answer key.

Chinese addresses are written in the reverse order to the way addresses are written in English. In English, you give the number of your flat/house first, then the street or road and then the town or city. In Chinese, it is city, street, number.

5 Follow the same pattern as the passage you heard in the listening activity and say something about yourself.

   a Fill in your details on the table. You can do this exercise even if you don't have the recording.
   b Think of one of your friends and fill in their details.
   c If you are doing this with another person, ask them questions and fill in their details.

	Yourself	Friend A	Friend B
Surname			
Given name			
Nationality			
Phone no			
Address			
– city			
– street			
– number			

6 You often see Chinese addresses written in English, as in the following examples. How would these addresses be said (or written) in Chinese?

   a Mingli Li (Lecturer)
      2, Chaoyang Lu
      BEIJING

   b Mr. Hua Zhao, Room 384, Dongfang Hotel, 9 Longhai Lu, Suzhou

   c Miss Jiabao Zhao,
      5, Heping Lu,
      Xicheng Qu,
      Nanjing

7 Match the words in the left-hand column with the ones on the right to make words you've already learnt.

a fēijī
b Lúndūn
c Hépíng
d èr-líng-wǔ
e míngtiān
f Dōngchéng
g diànhuà

1 Fàndiàn
2 jiàn
3 piào
4 Qū
5 fángjiān
6 hàomǎ
7 rén

Test yourself

1 03.10 **Now you've arrived at the end of Unit 3. How do you do the following?**

a You meet someone you don't know. How do you ask your friend who he is?
b Ask someone where they live?
c Tell someone that you don't live in London.
d Ask someone to give you their phone number.
e Ask what the meaning of **diànhuà** is.
f Say to the Chinese flight attendant that this is your (plane) ticket.

2 Vocabulary and pronunciation

a The Chinese for good is hǎo. What is the Chinese for *number*?
b Put the tone marks on Lundun.
c Is the sound for country guó or góu?
d What is the meaning of yìsi?

You'll find the answers in the Answer key. How have you done? If most of them are correct, you will be ready to go on to Unit 4. Congratulations! Before you do so, spend some time revising Units 1, 2 and 3. Regular revision will help to consolidate what you have learnt and give you more confidence.

SELF CHECK

I CAN...
...say where I come from and what nationality I am.
...ask for and give an address.
...say the numbers 0–10.
...ask for, and give, a phone number.
...fill out a form.

 KEY CHARACTERS

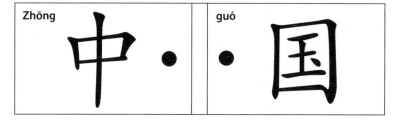

These two characters mean *centre* or *middle* and *country* or *state* respectively. Together they represent the word for *China*. Another name for China was the Middle Kingdom. Traditionally China saw itself as at the centre of the world, hence the name.

4

In this unit you will learn how to:
» talk about yourself and your family.
» ask other people about their family.
» say how old you are.
» ask how old somebody is.
» count up to 100.

Nǐ yǒu xiōngdì jiěmèi ma?

My progress tracker

Privacy

Among close Chinese friends the topics of conversation may be unlimited. Don't be embarrassed by this: as a matter of fact, no one is especially interested in your personal life – they just want to show you that they care about you by asking such questions. You don't have to respond accurately or in detail when asked questions such as **Chī fàn le ma?** (*Have you eaten?*) or **Nǐ qù nǎr?** (*Where are you going?*).

You'll find that speaking about yourself and your family in Chinese can be very easy. Remember how to say *I have* or *I don't have* (**wǒ yǒu, wǒ méi yǒu**)? This, together with the basic vocabulary you will learn in this unit, should give you all the tools you need!

However, describing your various relatives in Chinese can be quite tricky. It is a lot simpler in English, which means that there are often no English equivalents for many of the Chinese terms. Only some of the basic terms

40

will be covered here. For example, when you want to tell people in Chinese about your brothers and sisters, you need to be very precise. Your brother or sister is normally either older or younger than you and you have to specify this information.

You will also be able to count up to 100 by the end of this unit. Having mastered one to ten in Unit 3 you will be surprised how easy it is. 11 is 10 + 1, 12 is 10 + 2, 20 is 2 × 10, 30 is 3 × 10, all the way up to 99 which is 9 × 10 + 9. There is a special word **bǎi** for *hundred* so 100 is **yìbǎi** (you have to use **yī** *one*).

1 What does it mean when a Chinese person asks you or another Chinese person Chī fàn le ma?
  a Have you eaten?
  b Where are you going?

2 From the statement 'when you want to tell people in Chinese about your brothers and sisters, you need to be very precise', you can safely predict that there are specific words in Chinese for elder brother, younger brother, elder sister and younger sister respectively. True or false?

3 Following the rule above about formation of numbers between 11 and 99, what is the Chinese for 15 and 50?

Vocabulary builder

FAMILY MEMBERS

04.01 Listen as you look at the words and phrases and repeat what you hear.

bàba	*dad, father*
māma	*mum, mother*
érzi	*son*
nǚ'ér	*daughter*
gēge	*elder brother*
jiějie	*elder sister*
dìdi	*younger brother*
mèimei	*younger sister*
xiōngdì	*brothers*
jiěmèi	*sisters*
dà dìdi	*the older one of the younger brothers*
xiǎo dìdi	*the younger one of the younger brothers*

1 Match up the Chinese words with their English equivalents.

- a māma
- b mèimei
- c jiějie
- d gēge
- e dìdi

1. elder sister
2. younger sister
3. elder brother
4. younger brother
5. mum, mother

NUMBERS 11–100

04.02

shíyī	11	shíliù	16	sānshí	30	bāshí	80
shí'èr	12	shíqī	17	sìshí	40	jiǔshí	90
shísān	13	shíbā	18	wǔshí	50	yìbǎi	100
shísì	14	shíjiǔ	19	liùshí	60		
shíwǔ	15	èrshí	20	qīshí	70		

2 Match up the numbers in Chinese with their English equivalents

- a shíbā
- b èrshí
- c jiǔshí
- d shísì
- e wǔshí

1. 90
2. 50
3. 18
4. 20
5. 14

> **LANGUAGE TIP**
> Practise saying 11 to 15: **shíyī, shí'èr, shísān, shísì, shíwǔ**. Then say 16 to 20: **shíliù, shíqī, shíbā, shíjiǔ, èrshí**. Then put them together: **shíyī, shí'èr, shísān... èrshí**. Do the same for 21 to 25, 26 to 30, and so on.

NEW EXPRESSIONS

04.03 **Look at the expressions that are used in the following dialogue. Note their meanings and repeat what you hear.**

dà	*big*
gè	*measure word*
hé	*and*
jié hūn	*to marry*
. . . jié hūn le ma?	*. . . married?*
. . . jǐ suì?	*How old . . . ?* (for children)
le	*grammatical marker*
liǎng	*two* (of anything)
. . . suì	*. . . years old; age*
yí ge . . . yí ge	*one . . . , the other*
niánqīng	*young*

Dialogue 1 Family survey

04.04 *Dīng Fèng is carrying out a family survey on the number of children each household has and Liú Fúguì (from the Miáo national minority) has agreed to answer a few questions.*

1. **Listen and follow the dialogue. How do you ask someone if they have any children or not?**
2. **How many children does Mr Liu have?**
3. **How old are they?**

Dīng	Nín jiào shénme míngzi?
Liú	Wǒ jiào Liú Fúguì.
Dīng	Liú xiānsheng jié hūn le ma?
Liú	Jié hūn le.
Dīng	Yǒu mei yǒu háizi?
Liú	Yǒu liǎng ge, yí ge érzi, yí ge nǚ'ér.
Dīng	Tāmen jǐ suì?
Liú	Érzi liǎng suì, nǚ'ér wǔ suì.

Tones on 'yī'

Yī (*one*) is a 1st tone when it is part of a number, such as **yī** (*one*), **shíyī** (*eleven*), **èrshíyī** (*twenty-one*). When it occurs before a measure word it is normally a 4th tone, for example **yì tiān** (*one day*), **yì běn shū** (*one book*), but it turns into a 2nd tone before another 4th tone, for example **yí suì** (*one year old*). In **yí ge háizi**, **gè** is said without a tone, although it is actually 4th, but it still carries enough weight to change **yī** into a 2nd tone.

Suì (*year of age*), **tiān** (*day*) and **nián** (*year*) all act as measure words and nouns combined (refer to Language discovery note 2 for an explanation of what a measure word is). Note that **yìbǎi** is *one hundred*.

MORE NEW EXPRESSIONS

04.05 **Look at the expressions that are used in the following dialogues. Note their meanings and repeat what you hear.**

bú kèqi	*you are welcome* (lit. *not guest air*)
... duō dà?	*How old ...?*
... duō dà niánjì?	*How old ...?* (respectful) (lit. *how old year record*)
jīnnián	*this year*
kěshì	*but*
xiàng	*(to look) like*
bú xiàng	*not to look (like) it*
xiǎo	*small*
zhēnde	*really*

4 Nǐ yǒu xiōngdì jiěmèi ma?

Dialogue 2 More questions for Mr Liu

04.06 *Dīng Fèng asks Liú Fúguì some more questions.*

1 By reading and listening to the dialogue can you find out whether Liú Fúguì has any brothers or sisters?

Dīng	Nín yǒu xiōngdì jiěmèi ma?
Liú	Yǒu liǎng ge dìdi, yí ge mèimei. Méi yǒu gēge hé jiějie.
Dīng	Nín dìdi, mèimei duō dà?
Liú	Dà dìdi èrshíliù, xiǎo dìdi èrshísì.
Dīng	Mèimei ne?
Liú	Mèimei èrshíbā.
Dīng	Hěn hǎo, xièxie nín.
Liú	Bú kèqi.
Dīng	Zàijiàn.
Liú	Zàijiàn.

2 How old are they?

Dialogue 3 Looking at a family photo

04.07 *Wú and Lù are looking at a photo of Lù's family.*

1 What is Wú's impression of Lù's family members?

Wú	Nǐ bàba、māma duō dà niánjì?
Lù	Bàba wǔshísān, māma sìshíjiǔ.
Wú	Bú xiàng, bú xiàng. Zhè shì nǐ mèimei ba. Tā zhēn niánqīng.
Lù	Tā jīnnián èrshí'èr.
Wú	Zhēnde? Tā jié hūn le ma?
Lù	Méi yǒu. Kěshì yǒu nán péngyou le.
Wú	O.

2 Look at the dialogue to find the words to complete the sentences.

   a Lù xiānsheng de bàba wǔshí _____.
   b Lù xiānsheng de māma sì _____ jiǔ.
   c Lù xiānsheng de mèimei jīnnián _____ shí'èr.
   d Lù xiānsheng de mèimei méi yǒu _____.
   e Lù xiānsheng de mèimei yǒu nán _____ le.

Language discovery

1 SENTENCES ENDING IN 'LE'

If you put the little word **le** at the end of a sentence, it shows that something has happened or has already taken place:

Wǒ jié hūn le.	*I'm married.*
Wǒ qǐng tā le.	*I invited him.*
Wǒ wèn tā le.	*I asked her.*

If you want to make a question, simply add **ma** or **méi** (*you*) to the end of a sentence. **Yǒu** is unstressed.

Nǐ jié hūn le ma?	*Are you married?*
Nǐ jié hūn le méi you?	*Are you married?*

If you want to say something has not happened, you use **méi yǒu** (*not have*) plus the verb:

Wǒ méi yǒu jié hūn.	*I'm not married.*
Wǒ méi qǐng tā.	*I didn't invite him.*
Wǒ méi wèn tā.	*I haven't asked her.*

The **yǒu** can be omitted.

1 What's the difference between the following two sentences?
  a Tā lái.
  b Tā lái le.

2 MEASURE WORDS: ONE OR TWO

In Chinese, something called a measure word or classifier has to be used between a number and the noun following it.

In English, you can say:

two children
three daughters
four books

But in Chinese, you have to put the measure word/classifier in between the number and the item:

two measure word/classifier *children*
three measure word/classifier *daughters*
four measure word/classifier *books*

liǎng ge háizi 　　*two children*
sān ge nǚ'ér 　　*three daughters*
sì běn shū 　　*four books*

Different measure words are used with different categories of nouns. For example, **běn** is used for books and magazines, whereas **zhāng** is used for rectangular or square, flat objects such as tables, beds, maps and so on, but it is not a true measure as to length or anything else:

wǔ běn zázhì 　　*five magazines*
liù zhāng zhuōzi 　　*six tables*
qī zhāng chuáng 　　*seven beds*

Gè is by far the most common measure word. It is used with a whole range of nouns which do not have their own specific measure word. When in doubt, use **gè**! The noun accompanying the number and measure word is often omitted when it is clear from the context what this is:

Nǐ yǒu mei yǒu háizi? 　　*Have you any children?*
Yǒu liǎng ge (háizi), yí ge érzi, 　　*Two, a son and a daughter.*
　yí ge nǚ'ér.

2 Can you fill in the blanks with appropriate measure words?

   a Wǒ yǒu sān _____ shū.
   b Tā mǎi yī _____ zhuōzi.
   c Shuí yǒu liǎng _____ dìtú (*map*)?

3 TWO FOR TEA!

Liǎng meaning *two of a kind* is used with measure words instead of **èr** (two), so *two children* is **liǎng ge háizi** and not **èr ge háizi**.

3 Fill in the blanks with the appropriate word: liǎng or èr.

   a yī, _____, sān, sì, wǔ...
   b Tā yǒu _____ ge jiějie.

4 HOW OLD ARE YOU?

When asking about the age of small children, you use **jǐ** (*how many*) when you are expecting a small number (generally less than ten) as an answer plus the word for *years (of age)* **suì**:

Háizi jǐsuì? 　　*How old is/are the children?*
Tā wǔ suì. 　　*Five years old.*

Note that no verb is necessary in such sentences. When asking teenagers or young adults how old they are you use **duō** (*how*) together with **dà** (*old/big*):

Nǐ duō dà?	*How old are you?*
Wǒ èrshí suì.	*I'm 20.*

Again, note that no verb is necessary.

When asking older adults how old they are, the phrase **duō dà niánjì** (lit. *how big year record*) is used:

Nǐ bàba、māma duōdà niánjì?	*How old are your mum and dad?*
Bàba wǔshísān, māma sìshíjiǔ.	*Dad is 53, Mum is 49.*

Bàba (*dad*) comes before **māma** (*mum*) in Chinese word order, as does **fùqin** (*father*) before **mǔqin** (*mother*)!

5 PUNCTUATION – WHEN IS A COMMA NOT A COMMA?

When it's a pause mark! In Chinese, if two or more items are listed together, a pause mark is used between the items and not a comma. A comma is reserved for longer pauses:

Wǒ yǒu liǎng ge dìdi, yí ge mèimei.	*I have two younger brothers and a younger sister.*
Nǐ bàba、māma duō dà niánjì?	*How old are your mum and dad?*

6 APOSTROPHE FOR CLARITY

To prevent you saying **nǚér** instead of making a pause between the two syllables **nǚ** and **ér**, the Chinese insert an apostrophe (') between the two, so it is:

nǚ'ér
shí'èr (not shíèr)
èrshí'èr (not èrshíèr)

7 BROTHERS AND SISTERS

The collective term for *sisters* (without saying whether they are older or younger) is **jiěmèi**, combining half of **jiějie** with half of **mèimei**. Similarly there is a collective term for *brothers* **xiōngdì**, although in this case a more literary term for *elder brother* is used:

Wǒ méi yǒu xiōngdì jiěmèi.	*I don't have any brothers or sisters.*

8 POLITE TALK

In Unit 1, when Mrs Green thanked Xiǎo Wáng he responded by saying:

Bú yòng xiè.   *Don't mention it./Not at all.*

He could also have said **Bú xiè**.

An equally appropriate response to *thanks* would be:

Bú kèqi.   *It's nothing./Not at all.* (lit. *not guest air*)

Chinese people tend to say *thank you* rather less than in the West so they feel obliged to respond when somebody says *thank you* to them.

4 When someone says xièxie nǐ, what would you say in response?
   a Bú yòng xiè.   **b** Bú kèqi.

9 THE CHINESE ZODIAC

The Chinese zodiac works in a 12-year cycle rather than in months as the Western one does. You probably know whether you are a Capricorn or a Leo or another sign, but do you know which animal year you belong to? The order is as follows:

Rat (shǔ)	2020	2008	1996	1984	1972	1960
Ox (niú)	2021	2009	1997	1985	1973	1961
Tiger (hǔ)	2022	2010	1998	1986	1974	1962
Rabbit (tù)	2023	2011	1999	1987	1975	1963
Dragon (lóng)	2024	2012	2000	1988	1976	1964
Snake (shé)	2025	2013	2001	1989	1977	1965
Horse (mǎ)	2026	2014	2002	1990	1978	1966
Sheep (yáng)	2027	2015	2003	1991	1979	1967
Monkey (hóu)	2028	2016	2004	1992	1980	1968
Cockerel (jī)	2029	2017	2005	1993	1981	1969
Dog (gǒu)	2030	2018	2006	1994	1982	1970
Pig (zhū)	2031	2019	2007	1995	1983	1971

Can you work out which animal you are? For instance, if you were born in 2000 you are a dragon, if you were born in 1998 you are a tiger (though it is important to point out that the Chinese Lunar New Year does not start on the 1st of January. Like Easter, New Year's Day varies from year to year so you need to take the date into account if your birthday is at the start of the year.) (but make sure you take the Lunar New Year into account).

THE CHINESE CALENDAR

In China, there are two different calendars in use. One is identical to the Western calendar and the other is the traditional or lunar calendar. Chinese calendars include both! In the example shown here, the lunar calendar is written in small print. As you may have guessed, 廿 is the shortened form of 二十. On which date does Chinese New Year begin?

星期日	星期一	星期二	星期三	星期四	星期五	星期六
	1 ⁷ 元旦	2 ⁸ 初八	3 ⁹ 初九	4 ¹⁰ 初十	5 ¹¹ 小寒	6 ¹² 十二
7 ¹³ 十三	8 ¹⁴ 十四	9 ¹⁵ 十五	10 ¹⁶ 十六	11 ¹⁷ 十七	12 ¹⁸ 十八	13 ¹⁹ 十九
14 ²⁰ 二十	15 ²¹ 廿一	16 ²² 廿二	17 ²³ 廿三	18 ²⁴ 廿四	19 ²⁵ 廿五	20 ²⁶ 大寒
21 ²⁷ 廿七	22 ²⁸ 廿八	23 ²⁹ 廿九	24 ¹/¹ 正月	25 ² 初二	26 ³ 初三	27 ⁴ 初四
28 ⁵ 初五	29 ⁶ 初六	30 ⁷ 初七	31 ⁸ 初八			

Chinese New Year starts on 24 January in this particular year.

Each animal year is said to possess certain characteristics. It might be fun to get hold of a book on Chinese astrology or do some research online and find out more about your particular animal.

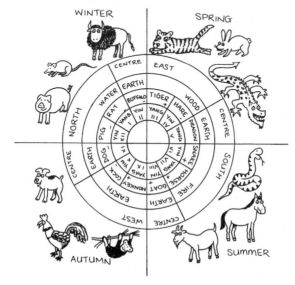

4 Nǐ yǒu xiōngdì jiěmèi ma?

Practice

1 **Choose the right number.**

   a Which is the smallest number?
   wǔshíbā   èrshíjiǔ   sìshíliù

   b Which is the odd one out?
   qīshíyī   bāshíbā   jiǔshíjiǔ

   c Which number is the largest?
   sānshí'èr   èrshísān   sānshíyī

2 **Find the number to replace the question marks and say it out loud in Chinese.**

   a $7 \times 3 = ?$
   b $? - 40 = 30$
   c $10 + ? = 76$
   d $98 \div 2 = ?$

   You can also say equations in Chinese:

   + jiā *plus*   × chéng *times*
   − jiǎn *minus*   ÷ chú *divided by*

   What would you say to fill these blanks?

   e Shíwǔ chéng èr shì _____.
   f _____ jiǎn wǔshí shì shí.
   g Èrshí jiā _____ shì sānshíwǔ.
   h Jiǔshíjiǔ chú sān shì _____.

3 **04.08 Listen to or read the following and say or write down the names and ages of Dīng's children. If you're still not sure of what you've heard, check the Answer key.**

   Dīng Fèng jié hūn le. Tā yǒu liǎng ge háizi, yí ge érzi, yí ge nǚ'ér. Érzi jiào Dīng Níng, jīnnián shí'èr suì. Nǚ'ér jiào Dīng Yīng, jīnnián shísì suì.

50

4 You are an only child and you are unmarried with no children. Your mother is a doctor (**yīsheng**), and your father is a teacher. How would you answer the following questions in Chinese?

a Nǐ yǒu gēge ma?
b Nǐ jié hūn le ma?
c Nǐ bàba shì yīsheng ma?
d Nǐ yǒu jǐ ge háizi?
e Nǐ dìdi jiào shénme?

5 Match the questions in the left-hand column with the answers on the right.

a Nǐ jié hūn le ma?
b Tā jǐ suì?
c Wáng lǎoshī jiào shénme míngzi?
d Nǐmen yǒu háizi ma?
e Lǐ tàitai yǒu nǚ'ér ma?

1 Wáng Yìfū.
2 Tā méi yǒu nǚ'ér.
3 Tā wǔ suì.
4 Wǒ jié hūn le.
5 Wǒmen méi háizi.

6 04.09 **Listen to what Hēnglì (*Henry*) says about himself and answer the questions.**

Wǒ jiào Hēnglì, jīnnián èrshí suì. Wǒ méi yǒu gēge, méi yǒu jiějie. Wǒ yǒu yí ge dìdi, yí ge mèimei. Wǒ dìdi jiào Bǐdé (Peter). Tā shíwǔ suì. Wǒ mèimei jiào Mǎlì (Mary). Tā jīnnián shíqī suì. Wǒmen dōu (all) shì xuésheng (student).

a How old is Hēnglì?
b How many brothers and sisters does he have?
c Are Hēnglì's brother(s) and sister(s) older or younger than him?
d How old are they?
e Are they working? What do they do?

7 **Now imagine you are Hēnglì's sister and talk about yourself and your brothers.**

Test yourself

04.10 Let's see how much you remember about Unit 4.

1 You see a little Chinese girl. How do you say the following to her:
   a Hello!
   b What's your name?
   c How old are you?
   d Have you got any brothers and sisters?
   e Thank you.
   f Goodbye!

2 Vocabulary and pronunciation
   a When you count two of something, do you use **èr** or **liǎng**?
   b What is the opposite of **dà**?
   c Who is older? Is it **dìdi** or **gēge**?
   d How is the Chinese for *and* pronounced: **hē**, **hé** or **hè**?

SELF CHECK

I CAN...
...talk about myself and my family.
...ask other people about their family.
...say how old I am.
...ask how old somebody is.
...count up to 100.

KEY CHARACTERS

 vs

Both 年 (**nián**) and 岁 (**suì**) mean *year*, but the usage is very different. While 年 is used in almost all cases to indicate *year*, the one exception is that it is NOT used to refer to a person's age. When we say someone is X years old, we can only use 岁 (**suì**). Be careful when you do use Chinese characters to write your age (e.g. on a form).

5

In this unit you will learn how to:
» say the days of the week.
» say the months of the year.
» tell the time.
» ask what time it is.
» say some useful expressions of time.
» give the date.
» make arrangements.

Jǐ diǎn le?

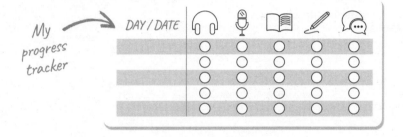

My progress tracker

The difference between 'nǐ' and 'nín'

Both **nǐ** and **nín** are pronouns meaning *you*. **Nǐ** is generally used to address people of your own age, people younger than you and close friends or acquaintances. **Nín** is used to address people older than you or higher up in the hierarchy than you to show respect.

OPENING HOURS IN CHINA

The regular working time is generally from Monday to Friday, with Saturday and Sunday off. Chinese people usually work between 08.00 and 18.00, with a lunch break from 12.00 to 14.00. Employees of official organizations such as government offices usually work from 09.00 to 17.00 with a one-hour break, and they do not work on Saturdays and Sundays.

Banks are usually open from 09.00 to 17.00 on weekdays (and for shorter hours on weekends). Hospitals and post offices are usually open from

08.00 until 17.00 every day. Shops, department stores and supermarkets are open every day from 08.30 or 09.30 to 21.30, including public holidays.

If you spend any time in China or another place where Chinese is spoken, you will need to be able to find out when shops and banks are open. You will also need to be able to recognize the Chinese characters for *opening times* (**yíngyè shíjiān**) 营业时间 and the numbers 1 to 12 (plus the characters for *o'clock*) and the days of the week. You will be able to do all this by the end of the unit.

Decide whether you would use nǐ or nín in the following situations:

1 At a conference where you are greeted by a Chinese person of roughly your own age (30s or 40s).
2 When meeting a Chinese delegation where you greet the head of the delegation who is about your own age (30s or 40s).
3 When addressing your Chinese teacher.

Vocabulary builder

TIME EXPRESSIONS

05.01 **Listen as you look at the words and phrases and repeat what you hear.**

diǎn	*o'clock*
fēn(zhōng)	*minute*
jǐ diǎn?	*what time . . . ?*
(Xiànzài) jǐ diǎn le?	*What time is it (now)?*
Jǐ yuè jǐ hào?	*What's the date?* (lit. *how many months, how many numbers?*)
shàngwǔ	*morning*
shíjiān	*time*
wǎnshang	*evening*
xiànzài	*now*
xiàwǔ	*afternoon*
xīngqī	*week*
Xīngqī jǐ?	*What day is it?*
yíkè	*a quarter* (time)
yuè	*month*
zǎoshang	*(early) morning*
zhōngwǔ	*noon*
zhōumò	*weekend*

5 Jǐ diǎn le?

1 Can you match the Chinese meaning to these English time words?

a early morning   1 wǎnshang
b morning   2 zǎoshang
c noon   3 xiàwǔ
d afternoon   4 shàngwǔ
e evening   5 zhōngwǔ

| Liǎng diǎn bàn | Sān diǎn yí kè | Chà wǔ fēn sì diǎn | Chà yí kè liù diǎn Wǔ diǎn sān kè |

MONTHS OF THE YEAR

05.02 Months of the year are very easy to say in Chinese. You already know the numbers 1 to 12. All you then need is the word for moon (**yuè**) 月. January is **yī-yuè**, February is **èr-yuè** and so on. Be careful not to confuse **yí ge yuè** *one month* with **yīyuè** *January*, **liǎng ge yuè** *two months* with **èryuè** *February*.

一月 yīyuè January	二月 èryuè February	三月 sānyuè March	四月 sìyuè April
五月 wǔyuè May	六月 liùyuè June	七月 qīyuè July	八月 bāyuè August
九月 jiǔyuè September	十月 shíyuè October	十一月 shíyīyuè November	十二月 shí'èryuè December

2 Now see if you can match the months in Chinese with their English equivalents.

a jiǔyuè   1 April
b sìyuè   2 June
c liùyuè   3 July
d qīyuè   4 September
e shíyuè   5 October

DAYS OF THE WEEK

05.03 Days of the week are also easy to say in Chinese. They all start with **xīngqī** 星期 (*week*) (lit. *star period*) and then you use the numbers 1 to 6 for Monday to Saturday. Sunday is special! You add the word **rì** 日 (*sun*) or **tiān** 天 (*day*) to **xīngqī** to make it into Sunday.

xīngqīyī	*Monday*	xīngqīwǔ	*Friday*
xīngqī'èr	*Tuesday*	xīngqīliù	*Saturday*
xīngqīsān	*Wednesday*	xīngqītiān	*Sunday*
xīngqīsì	*Thursday*	(or xīngqīrì)	

3 Now see if you can match the days of the week in Chinese with their English equivalents.

- **a** xīngqī'èr
- **b** xīngqīwǔ
- **c** xīngqītiān
- **d** xīngqīsì

1 Tuesday
2 Thursday
3 Friday
4 Sunday

05.03 Repeat the days of the week and the months of the year several times out loud until you have mastered them or listen to them on the recording and say them after the speaker.

NEW EXPRESSIONS: TIMES AND PLACES

05.04 Listen as you read the words and phrases and repeat what you hear.

bàn	*half*
chāoshì	*supermarket*
dào	*to*
dōu	*all, both*
guān (mén)	*to close (a door)*
hái...(ne)	*still*
Hépíng Chāoshì	*Peace Supermarket*
huì	*meeting*
jǐ?	*how many?* (usually less than ten)
kāi huì	*to have a meeting*
kāi (mén)	*to open (a door)*
kāishǐ	*to start*
wéi	*hello* (on phone)
yǐjīng	*already*
yǐwéi	*thought, to assume*

4 The following words on the left all start with the component **kāi** (meaning *to begin* or *to start*). Can you match each one with its correct English meaning?

a kāi-huì
b kāi-mén
c kāishǐ

1 to start
2 to have a meeting
3 to open a door

Dialogue 1 A customer rings a shop

05.05

1 When are the opening hours?

营业时间
星期一至星期五
08.00-17.30
星期六、星期日
09.00-17.00
Yíngyè shíjiān
Opening hours

Assistant	Wéi, Hépíng Chāoshì, nín hǎo?
Customer	Qǐng wèn, nǐmen jǐ diǎn kāi mén?
Assistant	Shàngwǔ bā diǎn dào xiàwǔ wǔ diǎn bàn.
Customer	Zhōngwǔ guān mén ma?
Assistant	Bù guān.
Customer	Zhōumò kāi bu kai?
Assistant	Xīngqīliù hé xīngqītiān dōu kāi.

早上　上午　中午　下午　晚上

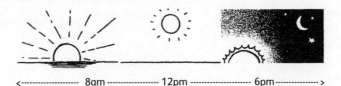

<----------- 8am ----------- 12pm ----------- 6pm ----------->

zǎoshang   shàngwǔ   zhōngwǔ   xiàwǔ   wǎnshang

Dialogue 2 Which day of the week is it today?

05.06 *Two colleagues, Xiǎo Xú and Lǎo Wàn, are in the office when Xiǎo Xú suddenly remembers something.*

1 What is it that he suddenly remembers?

Xiǎo Xú	Xiànzài jǐ diǎn le?
Lǎo Wàn	Liǎng diǎn yí kè le.
Xiǎo Xú	O, huì yǐjīng kāishǐ le.
Lǎo Wàn	Shénme huì? Nǐ bú shì míngtiān kāi huì ma?
Xiǎo Xú	Jīntiān xīngqī jǐ?
Lǎo Wàn	Xīngqīsān.
Xiǎo Xú	O, wǒ hái yǐwéi shì xīngqīsì ne.

2 What day did the conversation take place?

In Chinese-speaking environments other than China, you may well hear the word **lǐbài** 礼拜 used instead of **xīngqī**. So *Monday* would be **lǐbàiyī** instead of **xīngqīyī**, *Tuesday* would be **lǐbài'èr**, and so on. The word **lǐbài** has certain Christian connotations as *to go to church* is **zuò (*do*) lǐbài**.

NEW EXPRESSIONS: SAFE JOURNEY AND HAPPY BIRTHDAY!

05.07 **Listen and repeat what you hear.**

bāng	help
chà	lacking, short of
Chūnjié	the Spring Festival
dì	(for ordinal numbers)
hái yǒu	still have, there are still
huǒchē	train
jiù shì	to be precisely; to be nothing else but
kàn(yi)kàn	to have a look
kěxī	it's a pity
liàng	measure word for things with wheels e.g. car, train, bicycle
Lìwùpǔ	Liverpool
míngnián	next year
qù	go
qǔxiāo	to cancel
shàng	on

5 Jǐ diǎn le?

shēngrì	birthday
xià	next
yònggōng	hard-working
zhàntái	platform
zhīdào	to know
zhù (ni)	to wish (you)
zhù nǐ yílù shùnfēng!	have a safe journey!

The following two words may sound a little similar. One of them means *to help*, the other *half*. Can you tell which one is which?   **a** bāng   **b** bàn

Dialogue 3 At the train station

05.08 At a train station, Selena sees Mǎ Tè looking at the departures and arrivals board, obviously very perplexed. She decides to help him if she can.

What is Mǎ Tè perplexed about, and how did Selena help him?

Selena	Nǐ qù nǎr?
Mǎ Tè	Wǒ qù Lìwùpǔ.
Selena	Jǐ diǎn de huǒchē? Nǎ ge zhàntái?
Mǎ Tè	Wǒ bù zhīdao. Wǒ de huǒchē qǔxiāo le.
Selena	Wǒ bāng nǐ kànkan. (looks at the notice board)
	A, xià yí liàng shì sān diǎn yí kè, zài dì-liù zhàntái.
Mǎ Tè	Xiànzài sān diǎn chà wǔ fēn, hái yǒu èrshí fēnzhōng.
Selena	Zhù nǐ yílù shùnfēng.
Mǎ Tè	Xièxie nǐ. Zàijiàn.

Dialogue 4 Chinese New Year

05.09 Ann wants to find out whether her birthday happens to fall on Chinese New Year. Read the dialogue and see if you can find the answer.

Ann	Míngnián Chūnjié shì jǐ yuè jǐ hào?
Friend	Èryuè shí'èr hào.
Ann	Zhēn kěxī. Wǒde shēngrì shì èryuè shíyī hào.
Friend	Méi guānxi. Yīngguó shíyī hào de wǎnshang jiù shì Zhōngguó shí'èr hào de zǎoshang.

Language discovery

1 TELLING THE TIME

Xiànzài jǐ diǎn (zhōng) le?   *What time is it?* (lit. *now how many points clock*)

To reply to this question you use the 12-hour clock in Chinese. **Zhōng** is normally left out except when asking the time or (as in English) on the hour where it is optional. The use of **xiànzài** is also optional.

11.00	**(xiànzài) shíyī diǎn (zhōng) le**
11.05	**(xiànzài) shíyī diǎn (líng) wǔ fēn le. Líng** (*zero*) is optional.
11.10	**shíyī diǎn shí fēn**
11.15	**shíyī diǎn shíwǔ fēn** or **shíyī diǎn yí kè** (*one quarter*)
11.20	**shíyī diǎn èrshí fēn**
11.25	**shíyī diǎn èrshíwǔ fēn**
11.30	**shíyī diǎn sānshí** or **shíyī diǎn bàn** (*half*)
1.35	**yì diǎn sānshíwǔ** or **chà** (*lack*) **èrshíwǔ (fēn) liǎng diǎn**
1.40	**yì diǎn sìshí** or **chà èrshí (fēn) liǎng diǎn**
1.45	**yì diǎn sìshíwǔ fēn** or **yì diǎn sān kè** (*three quarters*) or **chà yí kè liǎng diǎn** or **liǎng diǎn chà yí kè**
1.50	**yì diǎn wǔshí fēn** or **chà shí fēn liǎng diǎn**
1.55	**yì diǎn wǔshíwǔ fēn** or **chà wǔ fēn liǎng diǎn**

Formal announcements of time are given using the 24-hour clock.

2 DATES

Months of the year, days of the week and parts of the day are easy (see earlier in this unit) but you still need to learn dates. In Chinese, the order for a date is the reverse of that used in English:

It is year, month, day, time of day (morning, afternoon, etc.), hour.

In Chinese, you move from the general to the particular.

The year is read as single numbers followed by the word **nián** 年 (*year*):

yī-jiǔ-yī-sì nián	*1914*
yī-jiǔ-sì-wǔ nián	*1945*

You ask what the date is by saying: **Jǐ yuè jǐ hào?** (lit. *how many months how many numbers*).

5 Jǐ diǎn le?   **61**

Jīntiān jǐ yuè jǐ hào?	What's the date today?
Jīntiān bāyuè shí hào.	Today's the 10th August.
Xīngqīsān jǐ hào?	What's the date on Wednesday?
(Xīngqīsān) èrshíbā hào.	It's the 28th (on Wednesday).

You can now work out how to say *12 noon on Tuesday, 23 July 1989*:

Yī-jiǔ-bā-jiǔ nián qīyuè èrshísān hào xīngqī'èr zhōngwǔ shí'èr diǎn.

Note that when you're telling the time and giving dates no verb is necessary. You have already met this in Unit 3 when dealing with ages.

3 ANOTHER TYPE OF 'LE'

You will have noticed the little word **le** appearing after **Xiànzài jǐ diǎn?** and **Liǎng diǎn yí kè** in Dialogue 2. It is used to indicate that a new state of affairs or situation has appeared. It is used at the end of such sentences as:

Nǐmen yǐjīng hěn dà le.	*You're already pretty grown up (whereas previously you weren't).*
Ta xiànzài (hěn) yònggōng le.	*She's very hard-working now (whereas previously she wasn't!).*

The Chinese stretch this idea of a change of state to its limits by often using it with questions and answers about age and time:

Háizi jǐ suì le?	*How old is the child?* (lit. *child how many years become*)
Xiànzài jǐ diǎn le?	*What time is it?* (lit. *now how many o'clock become*)

4 LINKING WORD 'DE'

This is the same **de** you saw in Unit 3. The main idea – what you are talking about – comes after the **de**, and what describes this main idea, or tells you more about it, comes before the **de**:

Jǐ diǎn de huǒchē?	*The train at what time?*
xīngqītiān kāi de shāngdiàn	*shops which open on Sundays*
zài Lúndūn kāi de huì	*the meeting held in London*

5 TICKET ON = ON THE TICKET

Piào shang (lit. *ticket on*) *on the ticket*. Here again it is the reverse of the English word order. Do the Chinese do everything back to front, you may be tempted to ask? No wonder they used to write from top to bottom and from right to left (and still do in Taiwan and Hong Kong)! Thus in Chinese you say:

shāngdiàn lǐ	*inside the shop*
lù shàng	*on the road/on the way*
huǒchē xià	*underneath the train*

Words such as **lǐ**, **shàng** and **xià** are normally unstressed when used in this way.

6 REPEATING THE VERB: 'KÀNKAN'!

Repeating the verb has the effect of softening the suggestion, question or statement. Thus the repeated verb is often unstressed. It conveys the idea of having a little go at doing the action of the verb, to try it out perhaps, or to do it without making a big fuss. Verbs of one syllable often have **yi** inserted in the middle when they are repeated.

Kànyikàn.	*Have a little look.*
Shuōyishuō.	*Try saying* (something); *Say a few words* (about something).

Verbs of two syllables cannot have **yi** inserted in this way; so you cannot say **rènshiyirènshi** or **kāishǐyikāishǐ**.

7 FIRST OR SECOND

To say *the first*, *the second*, and so on, you simply put the word **dì** in front of the number *one*, *two*, etc. **Èr** does not change into **liǎng** in such cases as there are not two seconds! An expression that used to be very common in China when any form of competition was involved is:

Yǒuyì dì-yī, bǐsài dì-èr.	*Friendship first, competition second.*

HAVE FUN WHILE YOU'RE LEARNING!

What have you learnt about the Chinese language so far? How is it different from any other language you've learnt? Take some time to reflect on this and jot down your thoughts. See if your ideas change as you learn more.

Practice

1 05.10 **Tongue-twisters are fun in any language. Try the following. Repeat them until you can say them off by heart:**

Sì shì sì.	4 is 4.
Shí shì shí.	10 is 10.
Sì bú shì shí.	4 is not 10.
Shí yě bú shì sì.	10 is not 4 either.
Shísì bú shì sìshí.	14 is not 40.
Sìshí yě bú shì shísì.	40 is not 14 either.

The last one is the hardest of all:

sìshísì ge shí shīzi　　　　　　　44 stone lions

2 05.11 **Can you say the dates of the following festivals (**jié**) in Chinese?**
   a New Year's Day (Xīnnián)
   b Christmas Day (Shèngdàn jié)
   c International Women's Day (Guójì Fùnǚ jié)
   d National Day of China (Zhōngguó de Guóqìng jié)
   e National Day of your country (X X de Guóqìng jié)

3 05.12 **You will hear some dates and times. Listen and repeat or read the dates and times and write them down in English.**
   a jiǔyuè jiǔ hào
   b xīngqītiān shàngwǔ
   c shíyīyuè èrshíbā hào xīngqīsì
   d xīngqīliù shàngwǔ shí diǎn sìshíwǔ
   e qīyuè liù hào xīngqīwǔ xiàwǔ sān diǎn bàn
   f shí'èryuè sānshíyī hào xīngqīyī shàngwǔ shíyī diǎn

4 Give the birthdays of five people using the following structures:

Sòng lǎoshī de shēngrì shì sìyuè shísì hào.
Sìyuè shísì hào shì Sòng lǎoshī de shēngrì.

5 Based on the assumption that the time is now 5.05 in the afternoon (xià wǔ wǔ diǎn líng wǔ fēn), answer the following questions in Chinese:
   a What will the time be in ten minutes?
   b What time was it ten minutes ago?
   c How long is it before it is 5.45?
   d What time is it in 12 hours' time?
   e The train is leaving in two minutes. What time is the train scheduled to leave?

6 Answer the following questions in Chinese.
   a What day is it tomorrow?
   b And yesterday?
   c Five days from today?
   d How many days is it before next Tuesday?

7 We don't know the answers to the following questions, but you do. Say your answers out loud in Chinese.
   a Which months are spring in the part of the world you are living in?
   b When is summer (i.e. what months)? Autumn? Winter?
   c How many months is it before your next birthday?
   d How many months is it before the New Year? (**Hái yǒu** X **ge yuè**.)

Test yourself

1 05.13 **Answer the following questions in Chinese, according to the information on the boards.**

Thursday 30 March
16.27
DEPARTURE
Cambridge
Platform 1
16.50

Thursday 30 March
16.27
ARRIVAL
Oxford
Platform 3
16.45

a What's the date today?
b What day is it today?
c What's the time now?
d When does the train from Oxford (**Niújīn**) arrive? At which platform?
e When does the train to Cambridge (**Jiànqiáo**) leave? From which platform?

2 Vocabulary and pronunciation
a What's the pronunciation for *all* or *both*? Is it **dōu** or **duō**?
b Which word means *morning*? Is it **xiàwǔ** or **shàngwǔ**?
c **Xīngqīsān** is *Wednesday*. What does **sān ge xīngqī** mean then?
d What is the difference between **sānyuè** and **sān ge yuè**?
e Do you know the meaning of **zhīdào**?

SELF CHECK

I CAN...

- ...say the days of the week.
- ...say the months of the year.
- ...tell the time.
- ...ask what time it is.
- ...say some useful expressions of time.
- ...give the date.
- ...make arrangements.

 KEY CHARACTERS

shàngwǔ   zhōngwǔ   xiàwǔ

These three 'words' (each made up of two Chinese characters) mean *morning*, *noon* and *afternoon* respectively. (You have already met 中 in 中国 (*China*) in Unit 3 meaning *middle* or *centre*.) In Chinese the 24-hour day is divided into 12 periods of 2 hours each. 午 is the 2-hour period of the day from 11.00 to 13.00 or 1 o'clock. So 上午 literally means *the period before* 午, 中午 means *the period between 11 and 13* and 下午 means *the period after 13.00 or 1 o'clock*. If the Chinese wish to say specifically *noon* i.e. 12 o'clock (on the dot), they say *12 o'clock after* 中午 i.e. 中午 shí'èrdiǎn. The Chinese think of time as a vertical concept with the earliest time (the past) coming at the top (上) and then descending (下). That might help you to understand why 上, 中 and 下 are also used when referring to volumes 1, 2 and 3 of a series.

Now to test you – if there are only two volumes to a book, which two characters would be used?

Review 1

Before you go onto Unit 6 let's do some revision exercises that relate more specifically to Units 1–5.

We'll start with Unit 1

 1 A Chinese visitor has knocked on the door of your office.
  a What would you call out?
  b How would you greet them when they come through the door?
  c How would you ask them to sit down?
  d At the end of your conversation you show them to the door. What do you say to them? (You have arranged to see them again tomorrow.)

Now for Unit 2

This exercise will show you how to briefly introduce yourself (or someone else) following the suggested patterns.

2 Name: **Wǒ jiào _____.** (Full name or just given name)
                       (Surname only: **Wǒ xìng _____.**)

3 Nationality: **Wǒ shì _____ rén.**

4 Profession/job: **Wǒ shì _____.**

(Use a dictionary or ask a Chinese friend for help if you need to.)

Now say these in one go. For example: **Wǒ xìng White. Wǒ jiào Peter (White). Wǒ shì Měiguó rén. Wǒ shì lǎoshī.**

Now for Unit 3

 5 You have just been introduced to a Chinese business associate who is on a week's visit to San Francisco.
  a Ask them which hotel they are staying in and what the number of their room is.
  b What do you say when you give them your name card?

Now for Unit 4

6 You are at a reception where you meet a Chinese acquaintance of a friend of yours. He does not speak any English so you take the opportunity to try out your Chinese. You know he is called Chén. Think of at least ten questions you can ask him in Chinese. Go back to Units 1 to 4 if you need to review vocabulary.

7 Revise the following numbers and say them out loud. 64 – 29 – 57 – 38 – 12 – 95 – 40 – 2 – 73 – 10. Check your answers with the section in Unit 4.

Now for Unit 5

8 You are in Běijīng and want to go to Tiānjīn in a couple of days' time. A Chinese friend offers to get your ticket for you as they know you are very busy. Tell them you want a train ticket for the 9.30 a.m. train on Thursday.

9 Say the following dates in Chinese:
 a 6 January 1997
 b 21 March 2020 (líng = zero)
 c 15 August 1943

10 When is your birthday?

11 When were your parents born?

If you have answered all these questions successfully then you are ready to go onto the second half of the course. If not, it would be a good idea to revise and consolidate what you have learnt so far before going onto Unit 6. It would also be a good idea to go back and reread the Learn to learn section at the front of the book where you will find many useful tips to improve your language learning skills.

6

In this unit you will learn how to:
» say what you want to do.
» understand and ask for advice.
» express similarities.
» compare and contrast.

Nǐ jīntiān xiǎng zuò shénme?

My progress tracker

Music

Chinese traditional music sounds very different from Western music. If you ever have the chance to see Peking opera, do take it. You may decide never to go again but it is certainly worth trying once, just for the experience! The make-up and costumes are very elaborate and give you all sorts of information about the characters being portrayed, so try to go with somebody who knows something about Peking opera. Most people enjoy the battles and the acrobatics if not the singing!

Examples of Peking opera masks

Exercise

You might have heard of **tàijí** (often written *Tai Chi* in the West) or **qìgōng**, forms of exercise practised for hundreds of years in China. Some forms of **qìgōng** are thought to be beneficial to people living with cancer and they are encouraged to go to regular classes (usually in the local park early in the morning around 6 a.m.) as part of their treatment and recovery programme.

Why not try out a Tai Chi or qigong class yourself? Look online for information. You are likely to meet other people in the class who are interested in learning Chinese and with whom you can practise, chat and exchange ideas.

The verbs that go with Tai Chi and qigong are different. Which verb do you think goes with which form of exercise?

   a zuò meaning *to do*   **b dǎ** meaning *to hit*

Vocabulary builder

WHAT DO YOU DO IN YOUR SPARE TIME?

06.01 Listen as you look at the words and phrases and repeat what you hear.

Běihǎi Gōngyuán	*Beihai Park*
chē	*vehicle (bus, bike, car)*
dìng (piào)	*to book (a ticket)*
dōngxi	*thing, object*
fúwùyuán	*assistant, housestaff (lit. service person)*
gěi	*for; to give*
huàn qián	*to change money*
kàn	*to watch, to look at*
mǎi	*to buy*
qián	*money*
ránhòu	*afterwards*
wèntí	*question, problem*
méi wèntí	*no problem*
xiān	*first*
xiǎng	*would like to; to think*
xiūxi	*to rest; rest*
yào	*to want; to need; will*
yínháng	*bank*

Leisure activities

06.02 Listen and repeat what you hear.

dǎ tàijíquán	*to do Tai Chi*
(kàn) diànyǐng	*film, movie*

6 Nǐ jīntiān xiǎng zuò shénme?

(kàn) jīngjù	*Peking opera*
(tīng) yīnyuè	*music*
yīnyuèhuì	*concert*
tīng yīnyuèhuì	*to attend a concert*
(kàn) zájì	*acrobatics*
zuò	*to do*
zuò qìgōng	*to do qigong*

QUESTIONS AND PHRASES

Shénme shíhou?	*When? What time?*
Zǎoshang hǎo!	*Good morning!*
zuò chē	*to take the bus* (lit. *sit vehicle*)
A bǐ B nán/róngyì	*A is more difficult/easier than B*
A gēn B (bù) yíyàng	*A is the same as (different from) B*
Nǐ xiǎng zuò shénme?	*What do you want to do?*
Tā zài zuò shénme?	*What's he/she doing?*
Tài hǎo le!	*Excellent!*

1 Match the verbs on the left hand side with the correct activity on the right hand side.

a	kàn	**1**	yīnyuèhuì
b	tīng	**2**	zájì
c	zuò	**3**	tàijí
d	dǎ	**4**	qìgōng

2 Here are two very useful speech patterns to do with making comparisons. We will see more about them in the next unit. For now, we need to be able to make simple statements with them.

Follow the first pattern **A gēn B (bù) yíyàng** and complete the Chinese translation for the following English sentences:

a Oxford and Cambridge are alike, both are very famous.
Niújīn _____ Jiànqiáo _____ _____, dōu hěn yǒu míng (*famous*, lit. 'have name').

b British English and American English are not the same.
Yīngguó yīngwén _____ Měiguó yīngwén _____ _____.

Follow the second pattern **A bǐ B (nán/róngyì)** and say:

c A is bigger than B.

d B is better than A.

Dialogue 1 Frank's plans

06.03 *Frank is attending a conference in China. Today he has a free day. His Chinese host, Xiǎo Wú, is asking him about his plans.*

Listen to or read the dialogue and note down his plans.

Shàngwǔ:	_____
Xiàwǔ:	_____
Wǎnshang:	_____
Xiǎo Wú	Jīntiān xiūxi. Nǐ xiǎng zuò shénme?
Frank	Wǒ xiǎng qù mǎi dōngxi. Kěshì wǒ yào xiān huàn qián.
Xiǎo Wú	Hǎo. Wǒmen xiān zuò chē qù yínháng huàn qián, ránhòu qù shāngdiàn mǎi dōngxi.
Frank	Hǎo. Xiàwǔ wǒ xiǎng qù Běihǎi Gōngyuán.
Xiǎo Wú	Méi wèntí. Wǎnshang ne?
Frank	Wǎnshang wǒmen qù kàn zájì hǎo bu hǎo?
Xiǎo Wú	Tài hǎo le. Wǒ qǐng fúwùyuán gěi wǒmen dìng piào.

NEW EXPRESSIONS

06.04 **Listen and repeat what you hear.**

háishi	or (used in question forms)
nàme	in that case, then
tīng	to listen to
Xīfāng	the West; Western
yǒu yìsi	interesting (lit. *have meaning*)

Dialogue 2 Frank

06.05 *Frank has changed his money, done the shopping and been to Beihai Park. Unfortunately there are no tickets for the acrobatics this evening. So Frank and Xiǎo Wú are planning what to do instead.*

1 What options have they considered?

Xiǎo Wú	Jīntiān wǎnshang nǐ xiǎng kàn diànyǐng háishi kàn jīngjù?
Frank	Wǒ bù xǐhuan jīngjù.
Xiǎo Wú	Nàme wǒmen kàn diànyǐng ba. Diànyǐng bǐ jīngjù yǒu yìsi.
Frank	Yǒu mei yǒu yīnyuèhuì?
Xiǎo Wú	Nǐ xiǎng tīng Zhōngguó yīnyuè háishi tīng Xīfāng yīnyuè?
Frank	Zài Zhōngguó dāngrán tīng Zhōngguó yīnyuè.

6 Nǐ jīntiān xiǎng zuò shénme?

2 What will they be doing instead in the evening?

> **TIP**
> Foreign credit and debit cards are only accepted in big department stores and hotels in China, not in ordinary shops. Chinese people use WeChat Pay or Alipay for almost everything. China is increasingly becoming a cashless society.

NEW EXPRESSIONS

 06.06 Listen and repeat what you hear.

bǐ	*compared to*
gēn	*and*
nán	*difficult*
róngyì	*easy*
yídìng	*certainly, definitely*
yíyàng	*same*
zài	*(indicating continuing action)*

3 There are many ways of learning words or vocabulary in general. One of the ways is to learn opposites. Now let's try practising some opposites that you have learnt. What do they mean?

  a yǒu wèntí; méi wèntí
  c yíyàng; bù yíyàng
  b yǒu yìsi; méi yìsi
  d nán; róngyi

4 Now try to fill in the blanks with the right word or phrase. Choose one of the two options in the brackets.

  a Wǒ bú huì shuō Zhōngwén. Zhōngwén tài _____ (nán; róngyi) le.
  b Tā bù xǐhuan jīngjù. Tā shuō jīngjù _____ (yǒu yìsi; méi yìsi).
  c Tā hé tā jiějie _____ (yíyàng; bù yíyàng). Tāmen dōu jié hūn le.

Dialogue 3 Early morning activities in the park

06.07 *A whole range of activities goes on in Chinese parks in the early morning. Frank decides to go and see for himself.*

What does Frank see in the park?

Frank	Zǎoshang hǎo!
Passer-by	Zǎoshang hǎo!
Frank	*(pointing to someone doing Tai Chi)* Tā zài zuò shénme?
Passer-by	Tā zài dǎ tàijíquán.
Frank	Nèi ge rén yě zài dǎ tàijíquán ma?
Passer-by	Bù. Tā zài zuò qìgōng.
Frank	Qìgōng gēn tàijíquán yíyàng ma?
Passer-by	Bù yíyàng.
Frank	Qìgōng bǐ tàijíquán nán ma?
Passer-by	Bù yídìng. Wǒ shuō qìgōng bǐ tàijíquán róngyì.

Language discovery

1 WORD ORDER AGAIN!

In some ways the Chinese language is less flexible than English in its word order. In English, you can say:

First I want to change some money.
or *I want to change some money first.*

In Chinese the position of **xiān** (*first*) is not changeable. It comes after **Wǒ yào** (*I want*) but before **huàn diǎnr qián** (*change some money*):

Wǒ yào xiān huàn diǎnr qián.

This is because **xiān** is connected with what you want to do, not with what you want; and adverbs like **xiān** precede the verb to which they refer.

2 WORD ORDER FOR ADVERBIAL PHRASES: TIME BEFORE MANNER BEFORE PLACE (TMP)

In Chinese you say:

I tomorrow at 9 a.m. (time) *by plane* (manner) *go to China* (place).

You can't say:

I'm going to China by plane at 9 a.m. tomorrow.
or *I'm going by plane to China at 9 a.m. tomorrow.*

In Chinese the word order is logical: first you establish when you're going to do it, then how you're going to do it, and then where you're going to do it. So the rule to remember is Time (T) comes before Manner (M) and Manner (M) comes before Place (P); TMP for short:

Wǒmen xiān (T) zuò chē (M) qù yínháng (P) huàn qián.
We'll go to the bank in the car to change money first (lit. we first sit car go bank change money).

Wǒmen shí'èr diǎn zhōng (T) zài Hépíng Fàndiàn (P) chī wǔfàn.
At 12 we'll have lunch at the Peace Hotel.

As you can see from the second example sometimes only two out of the three elements (TMP) are present but the rule still applies.

3 EXPRESSING ALTERNATIVES: EITHER . . . OR?

Do you want to go to a film or to the opera?

To express the *or* in the sentence above you use **háishi** in Chinese. Of course, you don't have to reverse the subject/verb order to make a question as in English.

All you need to do is put **háishi** between two statements thereby making them alternatives from which the listener must choose one:

Nǐ xiǎng kàn diànyǐng háishi kàn jīngjù?	*Would you like to go to a film or to the Peking opera?* (lit. *you fancy see film or see Peking opera*)
Nǐ xiǎng tīng Zhōngguó yīnyuè háishi (tīng) Xīfāng yīnyuè?	*Would you like to listen to Chinese music or Western music?*

If the subject or object in both halves is the same you don't need to repeat it (this holds true for any two clauses, not just ones using **háishi**, and is a feature of Chinese), but there should be a verb in both halves even if it is the same one. However, in colloquial Chinese the second verb is sometimes left out if it is the same as the first one. This is shown in the two earlier examples.

An exception to this rule is if the verb is **shì** (*to be*). In this case, the second **shì** may be left out. Here is an example of this:

Tā shì nǐde péngyou háishi nǐde lǎoshī?	*Is he your friend or your teacher?*

Try saying **háishi shì** and you'll understand why!

4 TO BE IN THE MIDDLE OF DOING SOMETHING

To show that an action is in progress the word **zài** is put in front of the verb:

Tā zài dǎ tàijíquán.	*He's doing Tai Chi.*
Wǒ zài zuò qìgōng.	*I'm doing qigong.*
Nǐ zài kàn diànshì.	*You're watching TV.*

You will sometimes find the words **zhèng** or **zhèng zài** used in exactly the same way instead of **zài**. They are simply alternatives. **Ne**, at the end of a sentence, can also convey the idea that the action is in progress; or you might find **ne** occurring with any of the above. Here are a few examples to illustrate this:

Xiǎo Liú zhèngzài tīng yīnyuè (ne).	*Xiao Liu is listening to music.*
Tāmen zhèng chī wǔfàn ne.	*They're in the middle of lunch.*
Wǒmen kāi huì ne. Qǐng nǐ míngtiān zài lái.	*We're in the middle of a meeting. Please come again tomorrow.*

Note that this action in progress can take place in the past, present or future and it is the use of time words (plus context) that tells us when the action actually takes place:

Míngtiān shàngwǔ tā yídìng zài yóuyǒng (ne).	*She'll certainly be swimming tomorrow morning.*
Zuótiān wǎnshang wǒ zài kàn jīngjù (ne).	*I was at the theatre yesterday evening.*

5 EXPRESSING SIMILARITY: IS IT THE SAME OR NOT?

In Chinese, to express that one thing is the same as another, or *A is the same as B* you say **A gēn** (*with*) **B yíyàng** (*the same*).

A gēn B yíyàng gāo.	*A is as tall as B.*
Wáng tàitai gēn Lǐ xiǎojie yíyàng gāo.	*Mrs Wang is as tall as Miss Li.*

To say that *A is not the same as B* you simply put **bù** in front of **yíyàng**:

A gēn B bù yíyàng gāo.	*A is not as tall as B.*
Wú xiānsheng gēn Szeto xiānsheng bù yíyàng gāo.	*Mr Wu is not as tall as Mr Szeto.*

6 MAKING COMPARISONS

To say that something is *more . . . than* use **bǐ**:

A bǐ B nán.	*A is more difficult than B.*
Qìgōng bǐ tàijíquán nán.	*Qigong is more difficult than Tai Chi.*
Kàn diànyǐng bǐ kàn jīngjù yǒu yìsi.	*Going to the cinema* (lit. see/watch film) *is more interesting than watching Peking opera.*

It is important to note that **bù bǐ** does not mean *less . . . than*. Look carefully at the following examples:

Tā bù bǐ wǒ dà.	*He is no older than I.*
Wǒ jiějie bù bǐ nǐ gāo.	*My elder sister is no taller than you.*

7 MODAL OR 'HELPING' VERBS

Verbs such as *want*, *ought to* and *must* can occur before action verbs or verbal expressions:

Nǐ xiǎng zuò shénme?	*What would you like to do?*
Wǒ xiǎng qù mǎi dōngxi.	*I'd like to go shopping.*
Wǒ gāi qù.	*I ought to go.*
Tā yào zǒu.	*She wants to leave.*
Nǐ huì shuō Hànyǔ ma?	*Can you speak Chinese?*
Tāmen xǐhuan mǎi dōngxi.	*They like shopping.*

Note the difference between **xiǎng** (*would like to do, fancy doing something*) and **xǐhuan** (*like*).

Unlike other types of verbs which can take endings to indicate, for example, that something has taken place or to show direction, these 'helping' or auxiliary verbs cannot have anything added to them.

8 TO GIVE OR NOT TO GIVE

Gěi basically means *to give*, but it can be used with a noun or pronoun (referring to a person or living thing) before the verb to mean *to do something for someone or something*.

Wǒ gěi nǐ kànkan.	*I'll take a look for you.*
Tā gěi wǒ kāi mén.	*He opened the door for me.*
Wǒ qǐng fúwùyuán gěi wǒmen dìng piào.	*I'll ask the attendant to book tickets for us.*

Practice

1 **Tā/tāmen zài zuò shénme?** *What is he/she doing? What are they doing?* Look at the pictures and say what the people are doing using the pattern above.

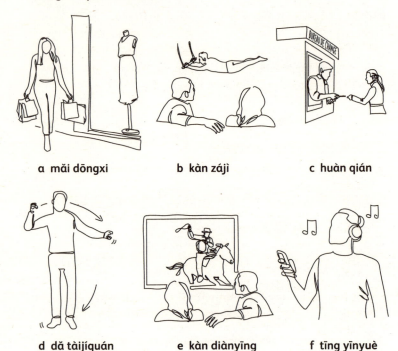

a mǎi dōngxi   b kàn zájì   c huàn qián

d dǎ tàijíquán   e kàn diànyǐng   f tīng yīnyuè

2 Look at the pictures in the previous exercise. Suppose these are the things you plan to do at the weekend. Draw up a plan and say when you are going to do what. Expressions of time can either occur before the verb, or at the beginning of the sentence if you want to give them more emphasis. Look at these examples:

Xīngqīliù shàngwǔ wǒ yào qù zuò qìgōng.
Xīngqītiān wǎnshang wǒ xiǎng qù kàn diànyǐng.

3 Tāmen yíyàng ma?

Are they the same?

gāo	tall
ǎi	short
dà	old
xiǎo	young (used when comparing ages)
zhòng	heavy

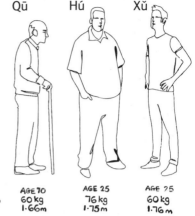

Answer the following questions using **yíyàng** or **bù yíyàng**.

a Qū gēn Xǔ yíyàng gāo ma?
b Xǔ gēn Hú yíyàng dà ma?
c Qū gēn Hú yíyàng zhòng ma?
d Xǔ gēn Hú yíyàng gāo ma?
e Qū gēn Xǔ yíyàng zhòng ma?
f Hú gēn Qū yíyàng dà ma?

4 According to the information in the previous exercise, are the following statements true or false? If true, say **duì**. If false, say **bú duì** and say what is true.

a Hú bǐ Xǔ gāo.
b Hú bù bǐ Qū zhòng.
c Xǔ bǐ Hú dà.
d Qū bǐ Xǔ dà.
e Hú gēn Xǔ bǐ Qū xiǎo.

5 The following is what Mr Hamid (Hāmǐdé xiānsheng) has put in his diary. Answer the questions below according to what is written in the diary.

Monday evening – learn Chinese
Tuesday morning – meeting
Wednesday morning – go to a concert
Thursday afternoon – meet a friend
Friday evening – see a film
Saturday – shopping
*   – change money*
Sunday – learn Tai Chi

6 Nǐ jīntiān xiǎng zuò shénme?

a Qióngsī xiānsheng xīngqīliù háishi xīngqītiān xué tàijíquán?
b Tā shénme shíhou qù kàn péngyou?
c Tā xīngqīsān shàngwǔ qù tīng yīnyuèhuì háishi xīngqīsì wǎnshang qù?
d Tā xīngqī'èr shàngwǔ kāi huì háishi xiàwǔ kāi huì?
e Tā shénme shíhou qù mǎi dōngxi?

Test yourself

1 06.08 **Say the following in Chinese.**
a Ask your Chinese friend what they would like to do tomorrow.
b Say Xiǎo Mǎ and her elder sister are as tall as each other.
c Say you find acrobatics more interesting than Peking opera.
d Ask Xiǎo Zhào where he would like to go this evening.
e Ask Miss Lǐ whether she would like to see a film or go to a concert.

2 Vocabulary and pronunciation
a You learnt **hé** meaning *and* in Unit 4. What is another Chinese word for *and* in this unit?
b **Háishi** means *or* only in: 1) question forms or 2) statements?
c Which phrase means *there is a problem*: 1) **méi wèntí** or 2) **yǒu wèntí**?
d What is the opposite of **róngyì**?
e Is the Chinese for *music*: **jīngjù**, **yīnyuè** or **diànyǐng**?

SELF CHECK	
	I CAN...
○	...say what I want to do.
○	...understand and ask for advice.
○	...express similarities.
○	...compare and contrast.

KEY CHARACTERS

The following signs should come in useful.

1 Now do you know what these two words **nán** and **nǚ**? mean?
2 Can you tell which of these two Chinese characters 女 男 means *man* and which one means *woman*?

In this unit you will learn how to:
» ask for things (in shops).
» ask the price.
» state quantities.
» say the numbers 100–1000.
» express the distance between two points.
» make more complex comparisons.

Duōshao qián?

Numbers

The Chinese like the number 8 (**bā**), because it sounds very like **fā** (发) meaning *to expand* or *prosperous*. As a result, phone numbers, car number plates etc. with an 8 in them are highly sought after and in some cases cost more, as people are so keen to have an 8 in their number that they are willing to pay for it.

The number 4 (**sì**), in contrast, is regarded as unlucky because it sounds very close to **sǐ** meaning *to die* or *death*. However, there is no need to be worried if there is a 4 in your phone number. Only a few people or businesses take it so seriously that they try to avoid the number 4 in daily life.

You may hear Chinese people say **gōng xǐ fā cái** (or **gung hay fat choy** in Cantonese) during the Chinese New Year period. Which word means *expand* or *prosperous*?

Vocabulary builder

GOING SHOPPING

07.01 Listen as you look at the words and phrases and repeat what you hear.

bǎi	*hundred*
búcuò	*pretty good, not bad*
jiàn	measure word for clothes
kuài	*unit of money*
lóu	*floor*
máoyī	*woollen sweater*
něi/nǎ?	*which?*
nèi/nà	*that*
shìhé	*to suit*
shìshi	*to try*
tài . . . le!	*too . . . !*
zhèi/zhè	*this*

FRUITS

07.02 Listen and repeat what you hear.

cǎoméi	*strawberry*
píngguǒ	*apple*
pútao	*grape*
xiāngjiāo	*banana*

COLORS

07.03 Listen and repeat what you hear.

hóng(sè) (de)	*red*
huáng(sè) (de)	*yellow*
lǜ (sè) (de)	*green*
lán(sè) (de)	*blue*
bái(sè) (de)	*white*
hēi(sè) (de)	*black*

7 Duōshao qián?

QUESTIONS AND PHRASES

07.04 Listen and repeat what you hear.

A lí B duō yuǎn?	How far is A from B?
A lí B hěn jìn/yuǎn.	A is close to/far from B.
Duō cháng?	How long?
Duō yuǎn?	How far?
Duōshao?	How much?/How many?
Duōshao qián yì jīn?/Yì jīn duōshao qián?	How much is it for half a kilo?
. . . kěyǐ ma?	Can I . . . ?/Is it allowed . . . ?
Nín mǎi shénme?	What would you like (to buy)?
Wǒ yào . . .	I want . . .
Shénme yánsè (de)?	What color?
. . . xíng ma?	Is it OK? Can I . . . ?
X zěnme mài?	How much is X?

NUMBERS 100–1000

07.05 Listen and repeat what you hear.

100	**yìbǎi**		300	**sānbǎi**
200	**èrbǎi** or **liǎng bǎi**		308	**sānbǎi líng bā**
202	**èrbǎi líng èr**		410	**sìbǎi yīshí**
210	**èrbǎi yīshí**		794	**qībǎi jiǔshísì**
225	**èrbǎi èrshíwǔ**		1000	**yìqiān**

Think of a number as being made up of units, tens and hundreds. If there is a zero in the tens column, you have to say **líng** (zero) in Chinese.

Ten is **shí** in Chinese but when it occurs with *one hundred*, *two hundred*, and so on you have to say *one ten*: **yīshí**, so *110* is **yìbǎi yīshí** (not **yìbǎi shí**).

Try saying the following numbers:

a 600
b 610
c 497
d 402
e 7000

Dialogue 1 Buying a sweater

07.06 *It may not be easy to get what you want in a shop despite the polite service you get. In this dialogue, the customer wants to buy a sweater.*

1 Listen to or read the dialogue and find out the following:
 a What options the customer was offered.
 b What reaction she had to each option.
 c What she finally bought.

(at the information point)
Customer Qǐng wèn, zài nǎr mǎi máoyī?
Assistant Zài èr lóu.
(at the knitwear counter)
Assistant Nín mǎi shénme?
Customer Wǒ xiǎng mǎi yí jiàn máoyī.
Assistant Yào něi jiàn? Nín xǐhuan shénme yánsè de?
Customer Nèi jiàn hóngsè de gěi wǒ kànkan xíng ma?
Assistant Zhèi jiàn hěn hǎo.
Customer O, tài dà le. Nèi jiàn huángsè de wǒ shìshi kěyǐ ma?
Assistant Zhèi jiàn yě búcuò.
Customer O, tài xiǎo le.
Assistant Zhèi jiàn lánsè de hěn shìhé nǐ.
Customer Tài hǎo le. Duōshao qián?
Assistant Wǔbǎi kuài.
Customer Ēn, tài guì le. Duìbuqǐ, xièxie nǐ.
Assistant ......

Did you get what the customer was offered? Yes, she first asked for and was shown a **hóngsè de** (*a red one*), then she tried a **huángsè de** (*a yellow one*) and finally she was offered a **lánsè de** (*a blue one*). What was her reaction to each of them? Well, the **hóngsè de** was **tài dà le** (*too big*). The **huángsè de** was **tài xiǎo le** (*too small*). The **lánsè de** was **tài hǎo le** (*perfect*), but **tài guì le** (*too expensive*). So in the end, she didn't buy any of them.

2 Let's practise asking if you can have a look at something or if you can try something. How do you say the following in Chinese?
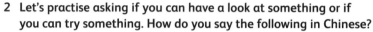
 a Can you let me have a look at X (please)?
 b Can I try X (please)?

3 Now let's practise talking about the quality or suitability of something. How do you say the following in Chinese?
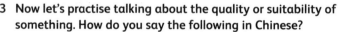
 a X is very good.   b X is not bad.   c X suits you.

7 Duōshao qián?   **87**

NEW EXPRESSIONS

07.07 Listen and repeat what you hear.

cái	not . . . until, only then
dào	to arrive, to go to
jǐ	crowded
jìn	near, close
jiù	just, only
kěshì	but
lí	distance from
shìchǎng	market
yuǎn	far
zánmen	we/us (including listener)
zhàn	(bus) stop, station
zhèr	here, this place
zìyóu	free, freedom
zǒu lù	to walk; on foot

Wǔxīng chāojí shìchǎng
Five Star Supermarket

LANGUAGE TIP
In Chinese, the *ground floor* is **yī lóu**, (lit. *one floor*), the *first floor* is **èr lóu** (lit. *two floor*), the *second floor* **sān lóu** (lit. *three floor*), the *third floor* **sì lóu** (lit. *four floor*) and so on.

Dialogue 2 Going to the free market

07.08 *If you can't get what you want in one shop, you can try somewhere else.*

Listen or read the dialogue and answer the questions.

  a Is the market far?
  b How can Fang and Ann get to the market?
  c How do they finally decide to get there?

Fāng	Wǒmen qù zìyóu shìchǎng kànkan ba.
Ann	Hǎo. Zìyóu shìchǎng lí zhèr duō yuǎn?
Fāng	Hěn jìn. Zuò chē liǎng、sān zhàn jiù dào le.
Ann	Chē tài jǐ le. Zánmen zǒu lù qù ba.
Fāng	Kěshì zǒu lù tài yuǎn le.
Ann	Zǒu lù yào duō cháng shíjiān?
Fāng	Zǒu lù èr、sānshí fēnzhōng cái néng dào.
Ann	Hǎo ba. Nàme zánmen zuò chē qù ba.

Buying fruit

07.09 Listen and repeat what you hear.

-deduō	much (more)
-duōle	much (more)
jīn	half a kilogram
mài	to sell
tián	sweet
xīnxiān	fresh
zhème (guì)	so (expensive)
zuì	the most

Dialogue 3 Bargaining

07.10 *There are markets throughout China where you can probably bargain. This is what you might hear at a fruit stall.*

1 **Listen or read the following dialogue and see how the buyer tries to argue the price down and how the seller tries to justify his prices.**

7 Duōshao qián? 89

Buyer	Píngguǒ zěnme mài?
Seller	Sì kuài yì jīn.
Buyer	Zhēn guì! Tāmende píngguǒ sān kuài bā yì jīn.
Seller	Kěshì wǒde píngguǒ bǐ tāmende dà yìdiǎnr.
Buyer	Pútao duōshao qián yì jīn?
Seller	Sì kuài liǎng máo wǔ yì jīn.
Buyer	Zhème guì! Tāmende sì kuài yì jīn.
Seller	Kěshì wǒde pútao bǐ tāmende tián duōle.
Buyer	Cǎoméi yì jīn duōshao qián?
Seller	Bā kuài èr.
Buyer	Tài guì le!
Seller	Kěshì wǒde cǎoméi bǐ tāmende xīnxiān deduō.
Buyer	Nǐde dōngxi zuì guì.
Seller	Kěshì wǒde dōngxi zuì hǎo!

Did you get it? In the conversation, the buyer either said that others' prices were lower, or simply said **tài guì le!** (*too expensive*). In response, the seller stated that his fruits were better.

2 Can you remember some or all of the sentences where a comparison is made? Go back and listen to the dialogue or read it again if necessary.
   a Wǒde píngguǒ bǐ tāmende dà yìdiǎnr.
   b Wǒde pútao bǐ tāmende tián duōle.
   c Wǒde cǎoméi bǐ tāmende xīnxiān deduō.

In the end, in response to the buyer's conclusion that **Nǐde dōngxi zuì guì** (*Your stuff is the most expensive*), the seller refuted this by saying **Kěshì wǒde dōngxi zuì hǎo!** (*but my things are the best*).

3 As in the previous unit, here is another exercise for practising pairs of opposites. In each case fill in the blank with the most appropriate word in Chinese from the pair in the brackets.
   a I want to buy a kilo of apples. Wǒ yào _____ (mǎi/mài) liǎng jīn píngguǒ.
   b She doesn't like that person. Tā bù xǐhuan _____ (zhè/nà) ge rén.
   c Is the market far? Shìchǎng _____ (yuǎn/jìn) ma?

斤斤计较 **Jīn jīn jìjiào** (Chinese proverb)
Haggle over every ounce, quibble over small differences

Language discovery

1 MORE ON MEASURE WORDS

You have already met the measure words **běn** (for books and magazines) and **zhāng** (for rectangular or square flat objects) in Unit 4, together with the most common measure word of all, **gè**.

Some measure words like **jīn** (*half a kilogram*) and **bēi** (*cup*) are actually indicators of quantity. The following table lists some of the more common of these:

Pinyin	Category	Examples
bǎ	objects with a handle, chairs	knife, umbrella, toothbrush, chair
bāo	parcel, packet	noodles, sugar
bēi	cup, glass	tea, coffee, wine
běn	volume	book, dictionary
fēng		letter
gè	people, things which do not fall into other categories; substitute MW	person, student
jiàn	piece, article	clothes, luggage
jīn	indicator of quantity (0.5 kilogram)	fruit, vegetables
kuài	piece	soap, land
lǐ	indicator of length (1/3 mile, 0.5 km)	road
liàng	things with wheels	car, bicycle
píng	bottles, jars	beer, wine, jam
tiáo	long and winding	towel, trousers, fish
wèi	people (polite)	teacher, lady, gentleman
zhāng	flat, rectangular objects	ticket, blanket, table, paper, map

Note that **gōngjīn** (lit. *public pound*) is a *kilogram*, **gōnglǐ** (lit. *public* **lǐ**) is a *kilometre* and **yīnglǐ** (lit. *English* **lǐ**) is a *mile*.

1 Fill in each blank with the most appropriate measure word.

   a yí _____ lǎoshī   **c** sān _____ shū (books)
   b liǎng _____ máoyī   **d** sì _____ jiǔ (wine)

2 MONEY, MONEY, MONEY . . . !

Chinese money is based on the decimal system and the currency in China is known as **rénmínbì** (*the people's currency*), often abbreviated to RMB. Foreign currency is known as **wàibì** (lit. *external/outside currency*).

The largest single unit is the **yuán** 元 (written as ¥ in many transactions). The highest value **yuán** note is 100 **yuán**. There are ten **jiǎo** 角 in one **yuán** and ten **fēn** 分 in one **jiǎo**. These are the words (and Chinese characters) used in the written language and printed on banknotes, tickets, etc. so it is important to recognize them. However, as we have said before, China is becoming an increasingly cashless society. Many transactions are conducted with 'tap to pay' systems on phones.

You saw how the characters for 1 to 10 were written in Unit 3. Don't be put off by the more complex characters you will see on Chinese banknotes. This also goes for the character 元 which is written 圓 on banknotes. These prevent confusion (and forgery!) when numbers are being written out in financial transactions.

In spoken Chinese, **kuài** 块 *piece/lump* is used for **yuán** and **máo** 毛 for **jiǎo** but **fēn** remains unchanged. (Although **fēn** is still used as a money unit and is still very much in the language, you are unlikely to see actual **fēn** coins.)

RMB	Spoken	Written
0.01 yuán	yì fēn (qián)	yì fēn
0.1 yuán	yì máo (qián)	yì jiǎo
1.00 yuán	yí kuài (qián)	yì yuán
5.5 yuán	wǔ kuài wǔ or wǔ kuài bàn	wǔ yuán wǔ jiǎo
14.32 yuán	shísì kuài sān máo èr	shísì yuán sān jiǎo èr fēn
30.09 yuán	sānshí kuài líng* jiǔ fēn	sānshí yuán líng* jiǔ fēn

* If a sum of money involves **kuài/yuán** and **fēn** but no **máo/jiǎo** the absence of **máo/jiǎo** is marked by **líng** (zero).

When two or more different units of currency are used together, the last one is often omitted:

sì kuài liù   rather than   **sì kuài liù máo**   ¥4.60
bā máo qī   rather than   **bā máo qī fēn**   ¥0.87

2 Say the following prices in Chinese.

Example: ¥ 4.03 sì kuài líng sān fēn

  a ¥0.52   c ¥12.76   e ¥205.54
  b ¥2.25   d ¥99.99   f ¥8.07

3 TOO MUCH?

Tài (*too*) is almost always used with **le**:

tài xiǎo le   too small
tài guì le   too expensive
tài hǎo le   excellent, great

It is probably better just to accept this as a rule rather than try to analyze it!

4 HOW FAR IS A FROM B?

To say *A is a long way from B*, where A and B are fixed points, use: A **lí** (*separate*) B **hěn yuǎn** (*far*).

If you don't use **hěn** (*very*), some sort of comparison is implied, i.e. *A is a long way from B (but near to C)*. Thus in Chinese, as we have said before, **hěn** is very weak.

Lúndūn lí Àidīngbǎo hěn yuǎn.   London is a long way from Edinburgh.

To say *A is near B* use: A **lí** B **hěn jìn** (*near*).

Niújīn lí Lúndūn hěn jìn.   Oxford is close to London.

To say exactly how far A is from B use: A **lí** B **yǒu** + the distance. **Yǒu** (*to have*) can also have the meaning *there is/there are*.

Jiànqiáo (Cambridge) lí Niújīn yǒu yìbǎiliùshí gōnglǐ.
Cambridge is 160 km from Oxford.

A and B can also be fixed points in time. To say how far A is from B in time use: A **lí** B **yǒu** + time difference.

Nǐde shēngrì lí jīntiān hái yǒu sì tiān.	*There are still four days to go to your birthday* (lit. *your birthday separate today still have four days*).

3 When you visit China, you may need to ask questions about how far a place is. Can you ask these questions in Chinese?

  a Is the market far?
  b How far is the market from here?
  c Is Beijing 100 kilometres from Tianjin?

5 APPROXIMATE NUMBERS

If you want to say *two or three (people)* in Chinese, you put the words for *two (of a pair)* and *three* one after another with a pause mark in between them:

liǎng、sān ge rén	*two or three people*
wǔ、liù běn shū	*five or six books*

20 or 30 is **èr、sānshí**: the **shí** is only said once.

45 or 46 is **sìshíwǔ、liù**: the **sìshí** is only said once.

4 Now try saying the following. Be careful with the measure word between the number and the noun.

  a six or seven kuài
  b 17 or 18 jīn (in weight)
  c 34 or 35 days

6 WE, INCLUDING YOU!

Both **zánmen** and **wǒmen** mean *we* and *us*. The difference is that **zánmen** specifically includes the listener(s) in what is being said.

Assaf says to his sister:

Zánmen bàba、māma duì wǒmen hěn hǎo shì bu shi?	*Our mum and dad were very good to us, weren't they?*

Zánmen here has a more intimate feel to it than **wǒmen**.

7 MORE ON COMPARISONS

You have already met **bǐ** in Unit 6:

Chī fàn bǐ hē jiǔ yǒu yìsi.   *Eating is more interesting than consuming alcohol.*

To say that *A is much more . . . than B* use:

A bǐ B adjective/verb **duōle** or **A bǐ B** adjective/verb **deduō**.

Zhè jiàn máoyī bǐ nèi jiàn dà duōle.   *This sweater is much bigger than that one.*

Cǎoméi bǐ píngguǒ guì deduō.   *Strawberries are much more expensive than apples.*

To say that *A is a little more . . . than B* use:

A bǐ B adjective/verb **yìdiǎnr**.

Wǒde shuǐguǒ *(fruit)* **bǐ tāde (shuǐguǒ) xīnxiān yìdiǎnr.**   *My fruit is a little fresher than his.*

5 Make comparisons with the information given using the pattern A bǐ B adjective or A bǐ B adjective (yìdiǎnr, deduō or duōle):

Example: cǎoméi ¥8.50/jīn, pútao ¥6.30/jīn =
Cǎoméi bǐ pútao guì duōle.

a Nǎ ge guì? (bǐ) jīn   Píngguǒ ¥4.00/jīn; Pútao ¥4.10/
b Tāmen shéi gāo? (yìdiǎnr)   Xiǎo Wáng 1.73m; Lǎo Lǐ 1.70m
c Nǎ ge dìfang rè (*hot*)? (duōle)   Běijīng 29°C; Lúndūn 17°C
d Tāmen shéi dà? (deduō)   Bái xiānsheng 58; Bái tàitai 48

8 SUPERLATIVES: BE THE BEST!

You only have to put the little word **zuì** (*most*) in front of **hǎo** to turn it into the best! Look carefully at the following examples using **zuì**:

zuì hǎo   *the best* (lit. *most good*)
zuì guì   *the most expensive*
zuì tián   *the sweetest*

You can put **de** + noun after the examples to make such phrases as:

zuì hǎo de pútao   *the best grapes*
zuì guì de cǎoméi   *the most expensive strawberries*
zuì tián de píngguǒ   *the sweetest apples*

9 ADVERBS 'CÁI' AND 'JIÙ'

Both **cái** and **jiù** are adverbs indicating something about time. **Cái** indicates that something takes place later or with more difficulty than had been expected. **Jiù**, on the other hand, indicates that something takes place earlier or more promptly than expected:

Tā sì diǎn zhōng cái lái.	*He didn't come until four (though I had asked him to come at 3.15).*
Tāmen liù diǎn bàn jiù lái le.	*They were there by 6.30 (though we had invited them for seven).*

Cái often translates as *not . . . until*. **Jiù** usually has a **le** at the end of the sentence to convey a sense of completion whereas **cái** does not. **Jiù** will sometimes have **zǎo** (*early*) in front of it as well as **le** at the end.

Both **cái** and **jiù** must come immediately before the verb whatever else there is in the sentence. Look carefully at the following examples:

Zuò chē liǎng、sān zhàn jiù dào le.	*It's only two or three stops on the bus.*
Zǒu lù èr、sānshí fēnzhōng cái néng dào.	*It will take as much as 20 or 30 minutes on foot (if we walk).*
Zuótiān hěn lěng dànshi jīntiān cái xià xuě.	*Yesterday was very cold but it didn't snow until today.*
Wǒ xiànzài cái zhīdao Fǎguó dōngxi guì.	*It's only now that I know things in France are expensive.*
Wǒ zǎo jiù zhīdao le.	*I knew ages ago (that things in France are expensive).*

6 Use either cái or jiù to fill in the blanks.

a Wǔ diǎn kāi huì, tā sì diǎn bàn _____ lái le.
b Nǐ hái bù zhīdao ma? Wǒ zuótiān (*yesterday*) _____ zhīdao le.
c Duìbuqǐ, Lǐ lǎoshī jīntiān bù néng lái. Tā míngtiān _____ lái.
d Tā bù xiǎng míngtiān qù, tā xiǎng xiànzài _____ qù.
e Yīnyuèhuì qī diǎn kāishǐ, tā qī diǎn yíkè _____ lái.

Most Chinese people are expert bargainers. A lot of selling is done from street stalls or with articles laid out on a piece of cloth on the ground. In these circumstances it is possible to bargain. If you are interested in buying something, point to it and say:

Zhè ge duōshao qián?   *How much is this?*

Having got a price, one way is to start by halving it and to say:

Wǒ zhǐ néng gěi nǐ X kuài.   *I can only give you X kuài.*

And then the fun starts with the two of you negotiating a price that you both find acceptable. It is a good policy to decide from the outset how much you are prepared to pay for something so that you have that in mind when bargaining. If neither of you can agree on a price, you can finish the bargaining by saying:

Xièxie, wǒ bù mǎi le.   *Thank you, I won't buy it then.*

and walking away. Sometimes if you are lucky, the vendor will rush after you and offer it to you for the last price you offered or one very similar.

Fruit and vegetables sold from stalls are normally offered at a certain price and if you think it's too expensive, you just don't buy them. Don't buy from anyone whose prices are not shown until you have ascertained how much they are. It is common for locals to be charged one price and tourists another (naturally more expensive). Unfortunately, it is very hard to check whether they are giving you the correct weight as they often use a pole with weights on one end and a pan (to hold the purchased fruit on) on the other.

There is no bargaining in ordinary shops and department stores.

Practice

1 Say the following prices in Chinese.

Example: ¥ 4.03 sì kuài líng sān fēn

a ¥0.52   c ¥12.76   e ¥205.54
b ¥2.25   d ¥99.99   f ¥8.07

2 Duōshao qián? *How much is it?*

Tell your Chinese friend how much these fruits cost in your local town. You need to know the words **yí bàng** (*pound*) and **biànshì** (*pence*).

Example: Píngguǒ wǔshíbā biànshì yì jīn.

Note that in prices over £1 that include pence, **shí** (*ten*) is left out where the number of pence is ten or more. The number of pence are treated as separate digits, for example, £1.45 is **yí bàng sì-wǔ**. One **jīn** (used all over China) is equivalent to half a kilogram or a little over a pound in weight.

3 You want to buy the following vegetables in a Chinese market, but they are not priced. Ask the greengrocer the prices by filling in the blanks in the questions:

xīhóngshì (*tomato*)   ¥3.50 a jin
báicài (*Chinese leaves*)   ¥1.72 a jin
tǔdòu (*potato*)   ¥2.28 a jin

a You   _____ mài?
  Greengrocer Sān kuài wǔ yì jīn.
b You   Yì jīn _____ qián?
  Greengrocer Yì jīn yí kuài qī máo èr.
c You   _____ qián yì jīn?
  Greengrocer Liǎng kuài liǎng máo bā yì jīn.

4 07.11 **Listen to the audio and write down the items mentioned and their prices. The first has been done for you. If you get really stuck look up the correct answer in the Answer key.**
   a yú (fish)   ¥7.09 jīn
   b   ¥
   c   ¥
   d   ¥
   e   ¥

5 **What would you say in the following situations?**

   Example: Situation – It's freezing today.
                You could say – **Jīntiān tài lěng** (*cold*) **le.**

   a You've tried on a sweater and found it too big.
   b It is 30°C today. (**rè** = *hot*)
   c She's got too much money!
   d A ticket to the match costs £150.
   e You have studied French for years and still cannot speak it (i.e. French is too difficult).

Test yourself

1 **07.12 How do you say the following?**
   a It will take only five minutes to get there.
   b It will take (as long as) 50 minutes to get there.
   c In my family my father is the oldest.
   d The cinema is not far from my home.
   e Bananas cost 49p per pound.

2 **Vocabulary and pronunciation**
   a What do the two words **jīn** and **jìn** mean respectively?
   b What do the two words **mǎi** and **mài** mean respectively?
   c What would be the measure word for *a coat*?
   d Put the tone mark on the word **bai** for *hundred*.
   e The pinyin for *to try* is: a) **shìshi** or b) **shìshì**?

SELF CHECK

I CAN...
...ask for things (in shops).
...ask the price.
...state quantities.
...say the numbers 100–1000.
...express the distance between two points.
...make more complex comparisons.

KEY CHARACTERS

Numbers: formal vs informal

In Language discovery note 2, we talk about 角 being used instead of 毛 and 元 being used instead of 圓 on banknotes and tickets. We also talk about more complex characters being used in such cases to prevent any confusion or forgery. Here are the 'simple' and 'complex' numbers for you to compare and slowly begin to recognize.

	'Simple' numbers	On bank notes
1	一	壹
2	二	贰
3	三	叁
4	四	肆
5	五	伍
6	六	陆
7	七	柒
8	八	捌
9	九	玖
10	十	拾

7 Duōshao qián?

8

In this unit you will learn how to:
» ask about sizes.
» talk about clothes and shoes.
» describe things.
» express likes and dislikes.
» make even more complex comparisons.

Zěnmeyàng?

My progress tracker

DAY / DATE	🎧	🎤	📖	✏️	💬
	○	○	○	○	○
	○	○	○	○	○
	○	○	○	○	○
	○	○	○	○	○
	○	○	○	○	○

Compliments

Even if your Chinese is very poor you will usually be told how good it is! The correct response to such compliments is either **Guòjiǎng, guòjiǎng** (*you praise me too much*), or **Nǎli, nǎli** (lit. *where, where?*, and meaning that you don't see it the way they do!). Young people in China tend to use a variety of expressions to show a certain degree of modesty such as **hái xíng** or **còuhe** (which roughly mean 'it's OK', 'not too bad' etc.) Self-deprecation is definitely a Chinese art – you are invited to somebody's house and the table is groaning with delicious food and you are told that it is only **biànfàn** (*simple/convenience food*). Examples such as these are endless and come under the general heading of **kèqi huà** (*polite talk*). Why not start making a list of them for your self?

1 When someone says **Nǐde Zhōngwén zhēn hǎo** (*Your Chinese is great*) to you, how could you respond?

2 When you say to a Chinese person **Nǐde Yīngwén zhēn hǎo** (*Your English is great*), you may hear them respond with **nǎlǐ, nǎlǐ**. What do they mean?

Vocabulary builder

BUYING CLOTHES

08.01 **Listen as you look at the words and phrases and repeat what you hear.**

dàxiǎo	size
hái kěyǐ	just so so
héshì	suitable
juéde	to feel, to think
mō(mo)	to feel, to touch
nánkàn	ugly
xīn	new
xīn mǎi de	newly bought
yánsè	color
yǒu yìdiǎn(r)	a little
zěnmeyàng?	how is it? how about it?
zhāng	measure word for flat objects
zhìliàng	quality
zhǐ yào	only need/cost
zúqiú	football

How good is it? We have learned quite a few expressions that describe the degree to which things have a certain quality. What do they mean?

1 hǎo
2 hái kěyǐ
3 búcuò
4 bù zěnmeyàng
5 fēicháng hǎo
6 bù hǎo
7 hěn bù hǎo
8 fēicháng bù hǎo

Dialogue 1 The new sweater

08.02 *Sùlán is showing her newly bought sweater to her boyfriend, Eli. She is very pleased with it as the price was reduced.*

But what does Eli think of the new sweater?

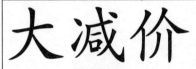

Dà jiǎn jià
Big reductions

Sùlán	Zhè shì wǒ xīn mǎi de máoyī. Nǐ kàn zěnmeyàng?
Eli	Búcuò, búcuò.
Sùlán	Dàxiǎo héshì ma?
Eli	Ēn, yǒu diǎnr dà.
Sùlán	Yánsè hǎokàn ma?
Eli	Ēn, bù nánkàn.
Sùlán	Nǐ mōmo. . . . Nǐ juéde zhìliàng zěnmeyàng?
Eli	Ēn, hái kěyǐ. Duōshao qián?
Sùlán	Bú guì, zhǐ yào yìbǎi wǔshí kuài.
Eli	Shénme?! Yìbǎi wǔshí kuài wǒ kěyǐ mǎi sān zhāng zúqiú piào!

NEW EXPRESSIONS

08.03 Listen and repeat what you hear.

bù zěnmeyàng	not so good
fēicháng	extremely
gèng	even more
guò	to pass or spend (time)
jiàqī	holiday, vacation
měi	every
měi tiān	every day
piányi	cheap
xià yǔ	to rain
Yìdàlì	Italy
yǐqián	before, in the past
zǎo jiù	ages ago; for ages
Zěnme le?	What is/was the matter?

Dialogue 2 Back from holiday

08.04 *Mr Li and Mrs Law are just back from holiday.*

1 Where did they each go for their holiday?

Mrs Law	Jiàqī guò-de hǎo ma?
Mr Lǐ	Fēicháng hǎo, jiù shi dōngxi bù piányi.
Mrs Law	Wǒ zǎo jiù zhīdao le.
Mr Lǐ	Wǒ yǐqián juéde Yīngguó de dōngxi guì, xiànzài cái zhīdao Fǎguó de dōngxi gèng guì.
Mrs Law	Yìdàlì de dōngxi yě hěn guì, shì bu shi?
Mr Lǐ	Yìdàlì de dōngxi yě bù bǐ Fǎguó de piányi. Nǐ de jiàqī guò-de zěnmeyàng?
Mrs Law	Bù zěnmeyàng.
Mr Lǐ	Zěnme le?
Mrs Law	Měi tiān dōu xià yǔ.

2 How was Mr Li's holiday?
3 How was Mrs Law's holiday?

NEW EXPRESSIONS

08.05 **Listen and repeat what you hear.**

kuài	*fast*	**xué(xí)**	*to learn, to study*
màn	*slow*	**yǐhòu**	*later, in future*
nǎli nǎli	*not really* (response to a compliment)	**Yīngwén**	*English language*
		zhǔyì	*idea*

Dialogue 3 A language exchange

08.06 *Martin is learning Chinese. He has met a Chinese person who is studying English.*

1 What is their plan?

Bǎojié	Nǐde Zhōngwén shuō-de zhēn hǎo.
Martin	Nǎli, nǎli. Wǒde Zhōngwén méi yǒu nǐde Yīngwén hǎo.
Bǎojié	Bù. Nǐde Zhōngwén bǐ wǒde Yīngwén hǎo deduō.
Martin	Yǐhòu wǒ bāng nǐ xué Yīngwén, nǐ bāng wǒ xué Zhōngwén, zěnmeyàng?
Bǎojié	Hǎo zhǔyì. Kěshì wǒ xué-de bú kuài.
Martin	Méi guānxi, wǒ xué-de yě hěn màn.

8 Zěnmeyàng?

Language discovery

1 A BIT . . . ?

To say something is *a little/bit* . . . use:

adjective + **(yì)diǎnr**

hǎo (yì)diǎnr *a bit better*
dà (yì)diǎnr *a little older/bigger*

(See also Language discovery note 7 in Unit 7, where adjective + **yìdiǎnr** is used in comparisons.)

When you wish to convey a negative feeling even if it is only subjective on your part, then **yǒu (yì)diǎnr** is put in front of the adjective:

Yǒu (yì)diǎnr guì. *It's a little on the expensive side.*
Yǒu (yì)diǎnr dà. *It's a bit on the big side.*

In all these examples, you can miss out the **yì** to sound more colloquial.

2 HOW WELL DO YOU SPEAK CHINESE?

When you are describing how the action of a verb is carried out, such as *quickly*, *slowly*, *well*, you use **de** after the verb and then the word for *quick*, *slow*, *good*, and so on.

You do not have to change them into adverbs as in English – *quick* → *quickly*, *good* → *well*.

Nǐde Zhōngwén shuō-de zěnmeyàng? *What's your Chinese like?*
Wǒde Zhōngwén shuō-de bù hǎo. *I don't speak Chinese well.*
Wǒ xué-de bú kuài. *I don't learn fast.*

This **de** is different from the **de** you met in Units 3 and 5 but they are written the same in pinyin and both are toneless. They are, however, represented by two entirely different Chinese characters.

When sentences of this kind have an object you can repeat the verb after the object, adding **de** to the second verb:

Wǒ	**xué**	**Zhōngwén xué-de hěn màn.**
subject	verb	object

(I'm learning Chinese very slowly.)

Tā kàn shū kàn-de hěn duō. *He reads a lot.*

Or you can miss out the first verb and have the object coming straight after the subject followed by the verb with **de**:

Nǐ Rìyǔ shuō-de zěnmeyàng? *What's your Japanese like?*
object
Wǒ Rìyǔ shuō-de bù hǎo. *My Japanese is not very good.*

1 How well do they do the following things? Answer each of the following questions using the information given in brackets.

Example: Xiǎo Zhǔ Fǎyǔ shuō-de zěnmeyàng? (*not at all well*)
Answer: Tā Fǎyǔ shuō-de bù zěnmeyàng.

a Lǐ xiānsheng Déwén (*German*) shuō-de zěnmeyàng? (*very well*)
b Zhāng tàitai jiàqī guò-de hǎo bu hǎo? (*not very well*)
c Cháo xiǎojie Yīngwén xué-de kuài bu kuài? (*extremely quickly*)
d Mǎlì yòng kuàizi (*chopsticks*) yòng-de zěnmeyàng? (*not at all well*)
e Hēnglì shuō Rìyǔ (*Japanese*) shuō-de hěn qīngchu (*clearly*) ma? (*very clearly*)

3 WHAT'S IT LIKE?

Zěnmeyàng (*What's it like? How?*) is a useful question word in Chinese. As you saw in Unit 2, with **shéi** (*who*) and **shénme** (*what*), question words appear in the same position as the word or words that replace them in the answer:

Nǐ kàn zěnmeyàng? *What do you think?*
Nǐ mōmo. Nǐ juéde zhìliàng zěnmeyàng? *Feel it. What do you think of the quality?*
Jiàqī guò-de zěnmeyàng? *How was your holiday?*
(Guò-de) bù zěnmeyàng. *Not very good/not up to much.*

Note the neat expression **bù zěnmeyàng** (*not up to much*) in response to a question containing the question word **zěnmeyàng**.

4 EVEN MORE!

To say *even more expensive* in Chinese, you only have to put the little word **gèng** in front of **guì**:

gèng guì *even more expensive*
gèng piányi *even cheaper, still cheaper*
gèng kuài *even quicker, even more quickly*
Tā bǐ wǒ xué-de gèng màn. *He learns even more slowly than I do.*

You will sometimes find **hái** (*still*) used instead of **gèng**, but the meaning remains exactly the same:

Nǐ bǐ tā xiě-de hái hǎo.   *You write even better than she does.*

2 Say the following in Chinese:
   a even better
   b even more quickly
   c even more suitable; to suit better

5 EVEN MORE ON COMPARISONS!

You have already met **bǐ** in Units 6 and 7. If you wish to say that something (A) is not up to a certain standard as represented by another person, living thing or object (B) use:

A méi yǒu B adjective/verb

Wǒde Zhōngwén (A) méi yǒu nǐde Yīngwén (B) hǎo.   *My Chinese is not as good as your English.*
Nǐde qìchē méi yǒu wǒde (qìchē) kuài.   *Your car is not as fast as mine.*

You will sometimes find **nàme** or **zhème** (*so*) in front of the adjective:

Zhè jiàn máoyī de dàxiǎo méi yǒu nà jiàn (máoyī de dàxiǎo) nàme héshì.   *This sweater doesn't fit as well as that one* (lit. *This MW sweater's size not up to that MW (sweater's size) so suitable*).

6 EACH AND EVERY!

Měi (*each/every*) is often reinforced by putting **dōu** (*both/all*) before the verb:

Měi tiān dōu xià yǔ.   *It rains/rained every day.*
Tā měi nián dōu qù Zhōngguó.   *He goes to China every year.*

In this example, it is clear that **dōu** has to refer back to **měi nián** rather than to **tā**, which is singular.

Tiān and **nián** don't need a measure word between **měi** and themselves because they act as measure words as well as nouns, but other nouns do:

měi ge jiàqī   *every holiday*   **měi jiàn máoyī**   *every sweater*

Note that the measure word between **měi** and **rén** is optional.

3 Say the following in Chinese. Be careful with the measure word between the number and the noun.
   a everybody
   b every apple
   c each sweater
   d every book

Never give Chinese friends white flowers. White is the color for mourning in China. Be circumspect with red, too – it's the color associated with weddings (the bride's dress is traditionally red, although with Western influence this is also changing). At Chinese New Year presents of money are given in little red envelopes (**hóng bāo**), and couplets expressing good luck and good fortune for the coming year are written on red paper and pasted on people's doors.

Fill in the blanks:

At Chinese New Year, adults usually give children a _____, which contains _____.

Practice

1 Match up the opposites.

a yǐqián
b dà
c guì
d hǎokàn
e kuài
f zǎo
g nán

1 nánkàn
2 màn
3 róngyì
4 piányi
5 yǐhòu
6 xiǎo
7 wǎn

NEW EXPRESSIONS: ITEMS OF CLOTHING

08.07 Listen and repeat what you hear.

Item	Measure word	English
chènyī	(jiàn)	shirt
dàyī	(jiàn)	overcoat
jiākè	(jiàn)	jacket
kùzi	(tiáo)	trousers
nèikù	(tiáo)	underpants
qúnzi	(tiáo)	skirt
shuìyī	(jiàn)	nightdress; pyjamas
xié	(shuāng)	shoes (a pair of)
xīfú	(tào)	suit (Western)
yǔyī	(jiàn)	raincoat

2 Refer to the list of colors in Unit 7 and items of clothing above. How would you ask for the following things in Chinese? (Note the measure words.)

Example: a green jacket **yí jiàn lǜ jiākè**

a a white shirt
b a yellow overcoat
c a blue suit
d a green skirt
e a pair of black shoes
f a pair of red trousers

NEW EXPRESSIONS: MATERIALS

bù	*cotton; cloth*
bùxié	*cloth shoes*
pí	*leather*
píxié	*leather shoes*
sīchóu	*silk*
rénzào gé	*imitation leather*

3 08.08 **Listen and answer the following questions, but before you do so, first look at the new expressions above. If you don't have the audio, read the passage and then answer the questions.**

DIFFERENT PEOPLE WEAR DIFFERENT CLOTHES

Xiǎo Cài jīntiān chuān (*to wear*) yí jiàn bái chènyī、yì tiáo lán qúnzi. Xiǎo Cài hěn xǐhuan chuān píxié. Jīntiān tā chuān yì shuāng hóng píxié.

Xiǎo Zhào jīntiān chuān yí jiàn lán de sīchóu chènyī、yì tiáo hēi kùzi. Xiǎo Zhào zuì bù xǐhuan chuān píxié. Tā jīntiān chuān yì shuāng lǜ bùxié.

Lǎo Fāng jīntiān chuān yí tào hēi xīfú、yí jiàn bái chènyī、yì shuāng hēi píxié. Xīngqīyī dào xīngqīwǔ tā dōu chuān xīfú hé píxié.

  a Xiǎo Cài jīntiān chuān shénme?
  b Xiǎo Zhào jīntiān chuān shénme?
  c Lǎo Fāng jīntiān chuān shénme?

4 Describe what the following people are wearing with the information provided:

  Example: Xiǎo Wáng/white shirt/black trousers/yellow shoes.
  Answer: Xiǎo Wáng chuān yí jiàn bái chènyī、yì tiáo hēi kùzi、yì shuāng huáng píxié.

  a Lǎo Mǎ/black leather shoes/blue shirt.
  b Xiǎo Qián/red shirt/black trousers/cloth shoes.
  c Liú xiānsheng/grey (**huī**) suit/yellow shirt/brown (**zōng**) leather shoes.

5 Look carefully at the pictures of Zhāng Tóng and Mǎ Fēng's cars and the sentences comparing their size and price. Then make up similar sentences comparing their height, age and weight, computers (**diànnǎo**) and handwriting (**zì**) using **méi yǒu** . . . and the adjectives given in brackets.

Zhāng Tóng's car (dà, guì)   Mǎ Fēng's car

Example: Mǎ Fēng de chē méi yǒu Zhāng Tóng de chē dà.
Zhang Tóng de chē méi yǒu Mǎ Fēng de chē guì.

Zhāng Tóng   Mǎ Fēng

a (gāo, dà, niánqīng)

Zhāng Tóng's computer   Ma Fēng's computer

b diànnǎo (*computer* but also used in conversation for *laptop*)
(dà, guì)

5 July Dear Jack, Weather here sunny and warm. Having a great holiday. See you soon! Zhang Tong	8/7. Hello Susan Raining again today. Why did I have to come to Scotland for my holidays? Miss you — Mm Feng

c zì (*handwriting*) (qīngchu *clear*)

Test yourself

1 08.09 **What do you say?**
   a Tell someone that they speak English very well.
   b Say that something, e.g. a shirt, is a bit small.
   c Ask someone how their holiday was.
   d Say that England (**Yīnggélán**) is smaller than Nigeria.
   e Say that Mexico is not as big as Brazil.

Bù gōngpíng   *Unfair*

2 Vocabulary and pronunciation
   a What do the two syllables stand for in the Chinese word **dàxiǎo** meaning *size*?
   b What is the opposite of **piányi**?
   c Which word means *slow*: a) **màn** or b) **kuài**?
   d Is the tone for the word *rain*: a) **yú**, b) **yǔ** or c) **yù**?
   e You want to say *later, in future*. Do you say: a) **yǐhòu** or b) **yǐqián**?

SELF CHECK

I CAN...
...ask about sizes.
...express likes and dislikes.
...talk about clothes and shoes.
...make even more comparisons.
...describe things.

KEY CHARACTERS

店 (pronounced **diàn**) *of all sorts*. **Diàn** means *shop* or *store*. There are quite a few words that have **diàn** as their last character. Here are some examples:

饭店   **fàndiàn** *restaurant* (literally *rice shop*)

饮食店   **yǐnshídiàn** *food and drinks shop* (literally *drinks and food shop*)

冷饮店   **lěngyǐndiàn** *cold drinks shop*

小吃店   **xiǎochīdiàn** *snack bar* (lit. *small eat shop*)

书店   **shūdiàn** *bookstore* (this one is obvious!)

9

In this unit you will learn how to:
» ask for and understand directions.
» say the points of the compass.
» use public transport.
» ask people if they have ever done something.
» express how long something happens for.

Qù . . . zěnme zǒu?

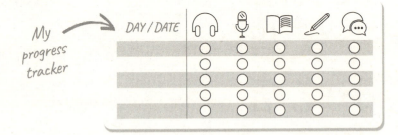

My progress tracker

Compass points

As China is situated in the East, the most important cardinal point is considered to be east rather than north. In the West we say north, south, east, west but Chinese people always start with **dōng** (east) and say either **dōng、nán** (south)、**xī** (west)、**běi** (north) or **dōng、xī、nán、běi**.

Southwest in Chinese is **xīnán** (west, south), *northeast* is **dōngběi** (lit. *east, north*) and so on. When giving someone directions, Chinese people (especially in the north) usually use the points of the compass rather than left and right. So it's good to know where north and south are when you ask somebody the way!

1 See if you can remember how Chinese people say the four directions.

   dōng, _____, nán, běi

 2 Say to a Chinese person that in the UK (or your own country) you would say the four directions in this way.

   běi, _____, dōng, xī

Vocabulary builder

09.01 Listen as you look at the words and phrases and repeat what you hear.

Àomén	Macao
chuán	ship, boat
cóng	from
dǎsuàn	to plan
dìfang	place
dù jià	to take a holiday
-guo	have ever (verb suffix)
jià	holiday
nàr/nàli	there (used interchangeably)
tiān	day
tīngshuō	I heard, I am told
tuìxiū	to retire
Xiānggǎng	Hong Kong
xiànmu	to envy
zěnme	how
cóng A dào B	from A to B
xiān . . . zài . . .	first . . . then . . .

1 Which word means *bus stop*?
  a chēzhàn
  b huàn chē

2 Which word means *to get on a bus*?
  a xià chē
  b shàng chē

3 Which word means *to go north*?
  a wǎng nán
  b wǎng běi

4 09.02 Now try saying these words which contain z and c.

zàijiàn, cóng, zěnme, cái, zuì, zúqiú

> **PRONUNCIATION TIPS**
> 1 **z** is pronounced like the *-ds* in *adds* or the *z* in *zoo*.
> 2 **c** is not at all like the *c* in English, so be very careful with it. It is pronounced like the *-ts* in *its*. It is useful to practise it together with **z** and to say them one after the other so that you can hear the difference clearly. Remember the top of your sheet of A4 should be blown away from you when you say **c** but not when you say **z**.

9 Qù . . . zěnme zǒu?

Dialogue 1 Talking about holidays

09.03 *Xiǎo Féng and Lǎo Qiáo are talking about taking their holidays.*

1 Where is Xiǎo Féng going and how will she get to those places?

Qiáo	Tīngshuō nǐ kuài yào qù dù jià le.
Féng	Duì. Wǒ yǒu sān ge xīngqī de jià, cóng liùyuè èrshíqī hào dào qīyuè shíbā hào.
Qiáo	Nǐ dǎsuàn qù nǎr?
Féng	Xiānggǎng hé Àomén. Zhèi liǎng ge dìfang wǒ dōu méi qù-guo.
Qiáo	Nǐ zěnme qù?
Féng	Wǒ xiān zuò fēijī dào Xiānggǎng, zài nàr zhù wǔ tiān. Zài cóng Xiānggǎng zuò chuán dào Àomén.
Qiáo	Wǒ zhēn xiànmu nǐ.
Féng	Nǐ shénme shíhou dù jià?
Qiáo	Wǒ? O, shí'èryuè.
Féng	Duō cháng shíjiān?
Qiáo	Bù zhīdao.
Féng	Zěnme huì bù zhīdao?
Qiáo	Jīnnián shí'èryuè wǒ jiù yào tuìxiū le.
Féng	Wǒ zhēn xiànmu nǐ.

2 What about Lǎo Qiáo? How long is his holiday?

NEW EXPRESSIONS: GIVING DIRECTIONS

09.04 Listen and repeat what you hear.

biān	side
-xībiānr	west side
-xīnán biānr	southwest side
chēzhàn	bus stop; train station
duìmiàn	opposite
huàn (chē)	to change (bus)
jiù	emphatic
kuài+verb...le	about to do something
X lù (chē)	the number X bus
mǎlù	road
méi shénme	it's nothing, don't mention it
qián	front; ahead

118

Tiāntán	Temple of Heaven
wǎng	in the direction of
wǎng nán kāi de chē	southbound bus
xià chē	to get off the bus
xíng	OK
yǐhòu	after
. . . jiù dào le.	It takes only . . . to get there.
Qù X zěnme zǒu?	How do (I) get to X?

Dialogue 2 Touring in Beijing

09.05 *Paola is touring in Beijing. Today she is going to visit Tiantan.*

公共汽车站

Gōnggòng qìchēzhàn *Bus stop*

1 Can you follow the directions given to her by a passer-by?

Paola	Qǐng wèn, qù Tiāntán zěnme zǒu?
Passer-by	Tiāntán zài xīnán biānr. Zuò chē sì zhàn jiù dào le.
Paola	Zuò jǐ lù chē?
Passer-by	Nǐ xiān cóng zhèr wǎng dōng zǒu, zài zuò wǎng nán kāi de chē, shíwǔ lù、èrshísān lù dōu xíng. Chēzhàn zài yínháng duìmiànr.
Paola	Yòng huàn chē ma?
Passer-by	Bú yòng. Xià chē yǐhòu wǎng qián zǒu yìdiǎnr. Tiāntán jiù zài mǎlù xībiānr.
Paola	Xièxie nín.
Passer-by	Méi shénme.

2 **Did you manage to follow the directions given to Paola by the passer-by? If you are still not quite sure, read or listen to the conversation again before you try answering the following questions.**
   a Tiāntán is to the _____ of where the speaker is.
   b They can take bus number_____ and bus number _____ to get there.
   c If they take the bus, it will take _____ stops.
   d When they get off the bus, Tiāntán is on the _____ side of the road.
   e If you face north, how do you tell someone in Chinese to turn east and west?

NEW EXPRESSIONS

09.06 Listen and repeat what you hear.

ānquán	safe
diànshì	TV
fā fēng	mad
fǎnzhèng	no way; in any case
gēn	with
háishi	would be better
jiā	home
lèi	tired; tiring
màoxiǎn	adventurous; to take the risk
pà	afraid
qí	to ride (bicycle, motorbike, horse)
qìchē	vehicle; bus; car
shūfu	comfortable
wēixiǎn	dangerous
xià ge	next
yào ...	it takes ...
yìqǐ	together
yòu ... yòu ...	both ... and ...
zhōumò	weekend
zìxíngchē	bicycle

Dialogue 3

09.07 *James is suggesting something adventurous to his friend, Huáng Zìlì.*

1 What is his suggestion and does Huáng accept it?

James	Nǐ qù-guo Tiānjīn ma?
Huáng	Méi qù-guo.
James	Xià ge zhōumò zánmen yìqǐ qù ba.
Huáng	Hǎo'a. Nǐ dǎsuàn zěnme qù? Zuò qìchē háishi zuò huǒchē?
James	Zánmen qí chē qù, zěnmeyàng?
Huáng	Shénme? Nǐ fā fēng le! Qí chē qù Tiānjīn yào liǎng、sān tiān, yòu lèi yòu wēixiǎn.
James	Wǒ bú pà lèi, yě xǐhuan màoxiǎn!
Huáng	Fǎnzhèng wǒ bù gēn nǐ yìqǐ qù. Wǒ zài jiā kàn diànshì, yòu shūfu yòu ānquán.

2 What was the 'adventurous' thing that James suggested?
 a That they walk.
 b That they cycle to Tiānjīn.

3 What was Huáng's reaction to it?
 a He thought James was mad.
 b He thought it was a good idea.

4 How long would it take them to get to Tiānjīn?
 a One or two days.
 b Two or three days.

5 Huáng's preferred option was:
 a yòu shūfu yòu ānquán
 b yòu lèi yòu wēixiǎn

Language discovery

1 ABOUT TO

To say something is about to happen or is going to happen soon use:

yào (*want, will*) + verb ... **le**

Nǐ yào qù dù jià le.	*You're going on holiday soon.*
Wǒ yào qù Xiānggǎng le.	*I'm about to leave for Hong Kong.*

Kuài (*quick*) or **jiù** (*then*) can also be put in front of **yào** to make the imminence of the action even clearer:

Jīnnián shí'èr yuè wǒ jiù yào tuìxiū le.	*I'll be retiring in December.*
Tā kuài yào kàn diànshì le.	*He's about to watch TV.*

1 How would you say the following:
 a The bus (**chē**) is about to come.
 b The bus is coming very soon.

2 FROM ... TO ...

Simply use **cóng** (*from*) and **dào** (*to*).

cóng Xiānggǎng dào Àomén	*from Hong Kong to Macao*
cóng Běijīng dào Tiānjīn	*from Beijing to Tianjin*

And from one time to another:

cóng sānyuè shíbā hào dào sìyuè jiǔ hào	*from 18 March to 9 April*

There are only two small points to remember.

The word order cannot be reversed in Chinese. You cannot say *I am going to* (**dào**) *China from* (**cóng**) *Japan*. So **cóng** must always precede **dào**.

In the sentence *I am going to* (**dào**) *Macao from* (**cóng**) *Hong Kong by* (**zuò**) *boat*, *from Hong Kong* must come first followed by the means of transport *by boat* and then *to Macao* last:

Wǒ cóng Xiānggǎng zuò chuán dào Àomén.

Chinese people are very logical – you cannot get to Macao unless you *sit on the boat* **zuò chuán** first so that should come before *to Macao* **dào Àomén**.

2 Say the following phrases:
   a from the UK to the US
   b from today to tomorrow
   c from this year to next year

3 PAST EXPERIENCE: HAVE YOU EVER . . . ?

If you put the little word **guo** after the verb it will emphasize a past experience:

Wǒ qù-guo Yìdàlì.	*I've been to Italy (at some time or other).*
Tā chī-guo Yìndù fàn.	*He has eaten Indian food (at some time in the past).*

You make the negative by putting **méi yǒu** in front of the verb:

Wǒ méi (yǒu) qù-guo Zhōngguó. *I have never been to China.*

You make the question by putting **ma** or **méi yǒu** at the end of the statement:

Nǐ qù-guo Tiānjīn ma?	*Have you (ever) been to Tianjin?*
Nǐ zuò-guo fēijī méi you?	*Have you (ever) travelled by plane?*
Hái méi yǒu (qù-guo).	*Not yet.*
Méi zuò-guo.	*No, never.*

Note the two possible ways of answering a question with **-guo**.

3 Have you ever ...?
   a Ask a Chinese person whether they have ever been to Germany.
   b Ask them whether they have ever learned German.
   c Ask them whether they have ever had German food.

4 SEQUENTIAL LINKERS: FIRST . . . THEN . . .

By using **xiān** (*first*) + verb followed by **zài** (*then*) + verb you show that the two actions are linked:

Wǒ xiān zuò fēijī dào Xiānggǎng, zài zuò huǒchē qù Běijīng.	*First I'll go to Hong Kong by plane then I'll go by train to Beijing.*
Nǐ xiān cóng zhèr wǎng dōng zǒu, zài zuò wǎng nán kāi de chē.	*You walk eastwards from here first. Then you get on a bus going south* (lit. *then sit towards south drive on bus*).

The **xiān** + verb and the **zài** + verb may occur in two separate sentences but the idea of sequence of actions is still there:

(Wǒ) xiān zuò fēijī dào Xiānggǎng . . . Zài cóng Xiānggǎng zuò chuán dào Àomén.	First I'll go to Hong Kong by plane . . . Then from Hong Kong I'll go to Macao by boat.

By the way, the Chinese character for this **zài** is written like the **zài** 再 in **zàijiàn** (*again*) not as in **zài** 在 (*at, in*).

4 Make the following suggestions.
   a Have a meal first and then go shopping.
   b Go shopping first and then watch a movie.
   c Learn Chinese first and then go to China.

5 DURATION: HOW LONG?

As you saw in Unit 1, time words like *today*, *Wednesday*, *6 o'clock* come before the verb in Chinese. However, when you want to say how long you do the action of the verb, the time word comes after the verb:

Wǒ zài nàr zhù wǔ tiān.	*I'll stay there five days.*
Tā zài zhèr gōngzuò le liǎng nián.	*She worked here for two years.*

The **le** after the verb shows that the action of the verb has been completed.

5 Answer the questions in Chinese.
   a Nǐ yào zhù jǐ tiān?
   b Nǐ xué le jǐ ge yuè de Zhōngwén?

6 'HUÌ' CAN

You met **huì** (*can*) in Unit 6 with the meaning *to know how to do something* (having learnt to do it). Its other meaning is *to be likely to* or *to be possible*:

Tā xiàwǔ huì lái.	*He'll (is likely to) come in the afternoon.*
Zěnme huì bù zhīdao?	*How could (you) not know?* (lit. *how possible not know?*)

6 Answer the questions in Chinese.
   a Jīnnián nǐ huì qù Zhōngguó ma?
   b Míngtiān nǐ huì qù mǎi dōngxi ma?

7 LINKERS: BOTH ... AND ...

To express *both ... and ...* you put **yòu** in front of the two adjectives or verbs:

yòu lèi yòu wēixiǎn	*both tiring and dangerous*
yòu shūfu yòu ānquán	*both comfortable and safe*
yòu hǎo yòu bú guì	*both good and inexpensive*

7 How would you say the following phrases in Chinese?
  a (It's both) good and comfortable.
  b bad and expensive
  c cheap and good

8 ADDED 'R'

You will find **r** added to some words in this unit so that you can get used to seeing and reading it. It is used a great deal by people in the north of China especially around Beijing. You certainly don't have to use it but it is important to know that it exists. It is to be found on the ends of words such as:

(yì)diǎn	**(yì)diǎnr**	*a little bit*
yì wǎn	**yì wǎnr**	*one bowl*
tiān	**tiānr**	*day*
duìmiàn	**duìmiànr**	*opposite*
biān	**biānr**	*side*
xībiān	**xībiānr**	*west side*
wán (verb)	**wánr**	*to enjoy oneself*

Practice

1 Answer the following *Have you ever ... ?* questions.

  Example: Nǐ qù-guo Zhōngguó ma? Qù-guo/Méi qù-guo.

  a Nǐ qù-guo Rìběn ma? (ever been to Japan?)
  b Nǐ zuò-guo fēijī ma? (ever travelled by plane?)
  c Nǐ kàn-guo Déguó diànyǐng ma? (ever seen German films?)
  d Nǐ chī-guo Zhōngguó fàn ma? (ever had Chinese food?)
  e Nǐ hē-guo Měiguó pútáojiǔ ma? (ever drunk American wine?)

9 Qù ... zěnme zǒu?

2 09.08 **Listen to the audio (or read the following passage) and draw the way to the cinema (diànyǐngyuàn) on the plan. Which letter represents the cinema?**

Xiān wǎng nán zǒu. Dào Dōnghǎi Lù zuò wǎng dōng kāi de chē. Zuò liǎng zhàn. Diànyǐngyuàn jiù zài Dōnghǎi Lù de nánbianr, shāngdiàn de duìmiànr.

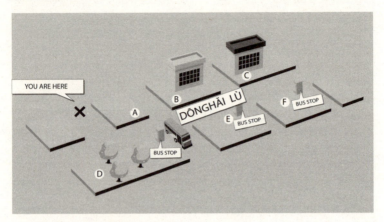

 3 **You are now in the cinema. You have just seen a film. Can you say in Chinese how you walk back to the hotel you are staying in (A)?**

 4 **Read the directions which tell you where various places are situated. Then go back to the sketch and identify the buildings represented by the letters B, C, D and E.**
   a Zhōngguó Yínháng zài diànyǐngyuàn de xībianr.
   b Shāngdiàn zài diànyǐngyuàn de duìmiàn.
   c Dōnghǎi Gōngyuán zài Zhōngguó Yínháng de xībian.
   d Xuéxiào (*school*) zài Zhōngguó Yínháng de běibian, fàndiàn de dōngbian.

5 Answer the following questions using **(cóng) ... dào ...** If you don't know, say **Wǒ bù zhīdao** (but you could find out).

Example: When is Mr Wang's next holiday?
(Cóng) wǔyuè sānshí hào dào liùyuè bā hào.

a When is your next holiday?
b What are the opening hours of your local (or school) library during the weekdays and weekends?
c Which days of the week do you work? (e.g. from Monday to Friday)
d What are your working hours during the week?

6 How do you get there? Choose an appropriate means of transport from the list to make complete sentences in Chinese, according to the information given in a–e. Take care with the word order!

zuò gōnggòng qìchē	by bus
zuò huǒchē	by train
zuò dìtiě	by underground
zuò fēijī	by plane
zuò chuán	by ship
qí (zìxíng)chē	to cycle
kāi chē	to drive
zǒu lù	to walk

Example: to go to work (qù shàng bān)
Wǒ qí zìxíngchē qù shàng bān.

a to go to work (qù shàng bān)
b to go to school (qù xuéxiào)
c to do shopping (qù mǎi dōngxi)
d to go to see a film (qù kàn diànyǐng)
    (at your local cinema)
e to go to X train station (qù X huǒchē zhàn)

9 Qù ... zěnme zǒu?   **127**

7 Here are some useful words to describe things. Which pair would you use to describe the following things? Try to use **yòu ... yòu ...**

Example: Zuò fēijī yòu guì yòu bù shūfu.
Zuò fēijī yòu kuài yòu shūfu.

guì	expensive	**bú guì**	not expensive
piányi	cheap	**bù piányi**	not cheap
fāngbiàn	convenient	**máfan**	troublesome
kuài	fast	**màn**	slow
wēixiǎn	dangerous	**ānquán**	safe

a Cóng Rìběn zuò chuán dào Zhōngguó.
b Zài Lúndūn/Bālí (*Paris*) qí zìxíngchē.
c Zuò gōnggòng qìchē qù shàng bān.
d Cóng Yīngguó zuò fēijī dào Měiguó.
e Kāi chē qù mǎi dōngxi.

8 **09.09** **Listen to the audio and answer the following questions about Mr White's holiday. See first if you can answer the questions in Chinese. If you find them too difficult, read the questions in English that follow and answer them either in English or in Chinese. If you haven't got the audio, read the passage after the questions and then answer the questions. If you need to refer to it, the English script is in the Answer key.**

a Bái xiānsheng dǎsuàn qù shénme dìfang?
b Tā zài Bālí zhù jǐ tiān?
c Tā gēn shéi yìqǐ qù Yìdàlì? Tāmen zěnme qù Yìdàlì?
d Bái xiānsheng dǎsuàn zài Yìdàlì zhù jǐ tiān?
e Tā zěnme huí Yīngguó?
f Tā péngyou zěnme huí Fǎguó?

a Where does Mr White plan to go?
b How long does he plan to stay in Paris?
c Who will he go to Italy with? How will they travel to Italy?
d How long does Mr White plan to stay in Italy?
e How will he get back to the UK?
f How will his friend get back to France?

BÁI XIĀNSHENG DE JIÀQĪ MR WHITE'S HOLIDAYS

Bái xiānsheng yào qù dù jià le. Tā yào qù liǎng ge dìfang. Tā xiān cóng Lúndūn zuò huǒchē dào Bālí. Tā dǎsuàn zài Bālí zhù sì tiān. Ránhòu tā gēn tāde Fǎguó péngyou kāi chē qù Yìdàlì. Tāmen dǎsuàn zài Yìdàlì zhù yí ge xīngqī. Zuìhòu tā cóng Yìdàlì zuò fēijī huí Lúndūn. Tāde péngyou kāi chē huí Fǎguó.

Test yourself

1 09.10 **Can you do the following?**
   a Ask how to get to the Bank of China (**Zhōngguó Yínháng**).
   b Tell the Chinese person who has asked you the way to take the number 10 bus.
   c Then tell her that it will be five stops (before she gets there).
   d Say that your friend has never been to China.
   e Say it's going to rain soon.

2 **Vocabulary and pronunciation**
   a What is the Chinese for Hong Kong?
   b **Nàli** means *there*. What is the other way of saying it?
   c What place is **Àomén**?
   d What does **cóng** mean?
   e Do *change money* and *change bus* share the same Chinese word for change?

SELF CHECK

I CAN...
...ask for and understand directions.
...say the points of the compass.
...use public transport.
...ask people if they have ever done something.
...express how long something happens for.

KEY CHARACTERS

Jìnzhǐ xī yān
禁止吸烟

禁止入内
NO ENTERING

As you can see, both warning signs start with the verb 禁止, which means *to forbid*.

The first notice 禁止吸烟 (**jìnzhǐ xī yān**) literally means *forbids inhaling smoke* i.e. *No smoking* and the second notice 禁止入内 (**jìnzhǐ rù nèi**) means *forbids entering inside* i.e. *No entry*.

10

In this unit you will learn how to:
» order a meal and drinks.
» pay the bill.
» say you have given up something (such as smoking).
» handle more verb endings.
» use more measure words.

Nín xiăng chī shénme?

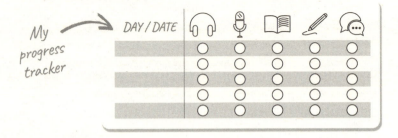

Eating at someone's house

The custom when eating Chinese food is that all the dishes are put in the middle of the table and shared. The host helps their guests to the best titbits. The soup is usually eaten last in China.

At a dinner, the most senior person or the host will sit in the chair that directly faces the door.

Here are some common phrases that people may use at a dinner table.

Gānbēi!	*Cheers* (lit. *dry glass*)!
Zhù nín shēntǐ jiànkāng.	*(To) your good health* (lit. *wish you body healthy*).

1 What would say when you propose a toast?
   a shēntǐ   b jiànkāng   c gānbēi
2 What is the most important seat at a dinner table?
   a The one facing the door.   b The one next to the entrance.

3 True or false?

a Chinese people tend to have the soup after the main course.
b It is regarded as rude for the host to select some food and put it on a guest's plate during the meal.

Vocabulary builder

10.01 Listen as you look at the words and phrases and repeat what you hear.

bēi	a cup of; cup
bié	don't
cài	dish
càidān	menu (lit. dish list)
Chángchéng	the Great Wall
chī	to eat
chī-wán/chī-bǎo/chī-hǎo le	to have finished eating/be full/satisfied
chī sù	to be vegetarian (lit. eat non-meat food)
duō	more; many
gēn wǒ lái	follow me
hǎochī	delicious, tasty
hē	to drink
là (de)	hot, spicy
pàng	overweight
rè	hot
shǎo	less; few
tiānqi	weather
yùdìng	to book (a room/table)
zhǐ	only
Nǐmen chī/hē diǎnr shénme?	What would you like to eat/drink?
Jiǔ lái le.	Here comes the wine.

FOOD AND DRINKS

10.02 Listen and repeat what you hear.

bīngqílín	ice cream
dòufu	beancurd
mápó dòufu	spicy beancurd/tofu
júzizhī	orange juice
pútáojiǔ	wine (lit. grape alcohol)
qīngcài	vegetables
ròu	meat

10 Nín xiǎng chī shénme?   133

tāng	soup
suānlà tāng	hot and sour soup
yú	fish
Qǐng wèn, yǒu ... ma?	Do you have...?; Is there any ... please?
quán sù de (shíwù)	vegan (food)
wú/méi yǒu táng de (yǐnshí)	sugar-free (food and drink)
wú/méi yǒu fū zhí de (yǐnshí)	gluten-free (food and drink)

Pronunciation

1 10.03 **Practise the difference between -uo and -ou as in duō (*much/many*) and dōu (*both/all*).**

2 **Practise the difference between -an and -ang as in fàn (*food*) and fàng (*to put*) and between -en and -eng as in fēn (*minute/smallest unit of Chinese currency*) and fēng (*wind*).**

3 **Now go back and revise all the vowels with a nasal sound in the Pronunciation guide. Listen to the audio if you have it.**

Hold your nose gently as you practise these sounds. You should be able to feel the vibration in it when you say **-ang**, **-eng**, **-iang**, **-ing**, **-iong**, **-ong** and **-uang**. This is particularly obvious when you say the sound in the 1st tone and hang on to it.

Dialogue 1 Eating with friends

Sìchuān cāntīng
Sichuan restaurant

10.04 *Mr Hussein and his friend Yúqiáo are going to have a Chinese meal.*

1 **What drinks and food have they ordered?**

   a Tick the drinks they ordered from this list:
   water _____, red wine _____, white wine _____, beer _____, juice _____, tea _____, coffee _____

   b Tick the food they ordered from this list:
   fish _____, beancurd _____, sweet and sour pork _____, vegetables _____

Server	Nǐmen yùdìng le ma?
Mr Hussein	Yùdìng le. Wǒ jiào Omar Hussein.
Server	Wǒ kànyikàn... Mr Hussein, qī diǎn bàn, liǎng ge rén.
Mr Hussein	Duì, duì.
Server	Hǎo, qǐng gēn wǒ lái...
Server	Zhè shì càidān. Nǐmen xiān hē diǎnr shénme?
Yúqiáo	Wǒ yào yì bēi júzizhī.
Mr Hussein	Nǐmen yǒu shénme pútáojiǔ?
Server	Wǒmen yǒu Chángchéng bái pútáojiǔ hé Zhōngguó hóng pútáojiǔ.
Mr Hussein	Lái yì bēi bái pútáojiǔ ba...
Server	Jiǔ lái le. Nǐmen yào shénme cài?
Yúqiáo	Wǒ bù chī ròu.
Mr Hussein	Nǐ chī bu chī yú?
Yúqiáo	Bù chī. Wǒ zhǐ yào qīngcài hé dòufu.
Mr Hussein	Shénme? Nǐ xiànzài chī sù le.
Yúqiáo	Shì'a. Wǒ yǐjīng hěn pàng le.
Server	Nǐmen xǐhuan chī là de ma?
Yùqiáo	Xǐhuan. Kěshì bié tài là le.
Server	Lái yí ge mápó dòufu ba.
Mr Hussein	Hǎo'a. Xiān lái liǎng ge suānlà tāng.
Yúqiáo	Jīntiān tiānqi yǐjīng hěn rè le. Wǒmen yīnggāi shǎo chī là de.
Server	Méi guānxi. Chī-wán fàn yǐhòu, nǐmen duō chī diǎnr bīngqílín. Wǒmen dē bīngqílín fēicháng hǎochī.

2 **Did they book a table?**
   a yes
   b no
   c not mentioned

3 **Who is a vegetarian?**
   a Mr Hussein
   b Yúqiáo
   c both of them
   d neither of them

4 **What was the weather like that day?**
   a hot
   b cold
   c not mentioned

10 Nín xiǎng chī shénme?

NEW EXPRESSIONS

10.05 Listen and repeat what you hear.

chá	*tea*
duì	*to; for*
kāfēi	*coffee*
mǎidān	*the bill please* (colloquial)
ràng	*to let, to allow*
shēntǐ	*health*
shōu	*to accept; to receive*
shuìjiào	*sleep*
Wèishénme?	*Why?*
xiànjīn	*cash*
yǐngxiǎng	*to influence; influence*
xìnyòngkǎ	*credit card*
zhī	*measure word for cigarettes*

Dialogue 2 What do you prefer to drink after an evening meal?

10.06 Mr Hussein and Yúqiáo are chatting at the end of their meal. Listen to or read their conversation and find out what they say about drinking coffee in the evening.

Mr Hussein	Hē bēi kāfēi ba.
Yúqiáo	Bù hē le.
Mr Hussein	Wèishénme? Wǒ zhīdào nǐ ài hē kāfēi.
Yúqiáo	Tài wǎnle. Wǒ pà yǐngxiǎng shuìjiào.
Mr Hussein	Wǒ bú pà. Nà nǐ hē bēi zhēnzhū nǎi chá bā?
Yúqiáo	Nà lái yībēi ba.... Zhēn hǎo hē!
Mr Hussein	... Nǐ chī bǎole ma?
Yúqiáo	Chī bǎole.
Mr Hussein	Wǒmen jié zhàng (*to get the bill*) ba. Fúwùyuán, mǎidān.
Server	Nǐmen chī-hǎo le ma?
Yúqiáo	Chī-hǎo le, xièxie.
Mr Hussein	Nǐmen shōu bù shōu xìnyòngkǎ?
Server	Duìbuqǐ, wǒmen zhǐ shōu xiànjīn.

* **zhēnzhū nǎi chá** *bubble tea*

1 **Who likes to drink coffee?**
   a Mr Hussein
   b Yúqiáo
   c both of them
   d neither of them
2 **Why did Yúqiáo not choose to drink coffee that evening?**
   a He doesn't like coffee.
   b He was in a hurry to leave.
   c It made him too sleepy.
   d It was a little too late to drink coffee then.
3 **What did Yúqiáo drink in the end?**
   a Chinese tea
   b English tea
   c bubble tea
   d juice
4 **In addition, from the conversation, we know that the restaurant accepts:**
   a cash only
   b credit card only
   c both credit card and cash
   d Chinese (Alipay)

CHOPSTICKS

When eating from street stalls or fast-food outlets you are usually given **wèishēng kuàizi** (*hygienic*, i.e. *disposable, chopsticks*), which should, of course, come wrapped. You have to break them apart, which shows you that they are still unused.

NEW EXPRESSIONS

 10.07 Listen and repeat what you hear.

è	*hungry*
chǎomiàn	*fried noodles*
fù qián	*to pay* (money)
-jíle	(suffix) *extremely*
kěkǒukělè	*cola*
shàng cì	*last time*
suàn-cuò le	*to have calculated wrongly*
suíbiàn	*casually*
tānzi	*stall*
tīng	*measure word for cans of drink*
wǎn(r)	*bowl*
yígòng	*altogether*

10 Nín xiǎng chī shénme?

Dialogue 3 At the street market

10.08 *Ann and Xiǎo Fāng have arrived at the street market (see Dialogue 3, Unit 7).*

Ann	Wǒ è le. Wǒmen suíbiàn chī diǎnr ba.
Fāng	Nàr yǒu ge xiǎo tānzi. Tāmen de chǎomiàn hǎochī-jíle.
	(At the food stall)
Fāng	Qǐng lái liǎng wǎnr chǎomiàn、liǎng tīng kěkǒukělè.
Server	Qǐng xiān fù qián. Liǎng wǎnr chǎomiàn wǔshí kuài, liǎng tīng kěkǒukělè shí kuài, yígòng liùshí kuài.
Fāng	Shénme? Nǐ suàn-cuò le ba. Shàng cì chǎomiàn èrshí kuài yì wǎnr.
Server	Méi suàn-cuò. Shàng cì shì shàng cì, xiànzài yì wǎnr èrshíwǔ kuài le.

1 **What did they do at the street market?**
   a They did some shopping.
   b They had some food at a food stall.
   c They saw people arguing over prices.
2 **What surprise did they find?**
   a They bumped into someone they knew.
   b The vendor recognized Fāng.
   c The price of the noodles they had has gone up.
3 **What did they eat and drink?**
4 **How much was the change in price of the food they had?**

Language discovery

1 ALREADY AND 'LE'

Remember using **le** in Unit 4 to show that something has happened or has already taken place? When **yǐjīng** (*already*) appears in front of a verb – or an adjective acting as a verb – it reinforces this idea of something having happened so you will find **le** at the end of such sentences:

Wǒ yǐjīng hěn pàng le.	*I'm already very overweight.*
Jīntiān yǐjīng hěn rè le.	*It's already very hot today.*

2 MORE BEFORE THE VERB!

To say *eat more*, put the little word **duō** (*much/many*) in front of the verb *to eat*:

duō chī   *eat more*

This works with all full verbs. It does *not* work with adjectives which can also act as verbs, such as **hǎo** (*good*), **pàng** (*overweight*) and so on.

duō hē	*drink more*
duō yào	*want more*
duō gěi	*give more*

You do exactly the same thing if you want to say *eat less, drink less*, and so on but you put **shǎo** (*less/few*) in front of the verb instead of **duō**:

shǎo chī	*eat less*
shǎo hē	*drink less*
shǎo yào	*want less*
shǎo gěi	*give less*

3 NOT ANY MORE!

To say that you don't do something anymore use **bù** verb (+ object) **le**:

Wǒ bù chī ròu le.	*I don't eat meat anymore/ I've given up eating meat.*
Wǒ dìdi bù chōu yān le.	*My younger brother has given up smoking/ doesn't smoke anymore.*
Yǐqián wǒmen shōu xiànjīn, xiànzài bù shōu le.	*We used to take cash, but we don't anymore.*
Tāmen bù niánqīng le.	*They're no longer young.*
Yǐqián wǒmen shōu xìnyòngkǎ, xiànzài bù shōu le.	*We used to take credit cards but we don't accept them anymore.*

If the verb is **yǒu** (*to have*), you have to use **méi** instead of **bù**:

Nǐ yǒu mei yǒu hóng chènyī?	*Do you have a red shirt?*
Méi yǒu le, mài-wán le.	*We're out of stock. They're sold out.* (lit. *Not have any more, sell finish* **le**.)

4 SMOKING IS NOT GOOD FOR YOUR HEALTH!

As you know, **duì** means *right, correct*. In certain contexts it also means *to* or *for*. Learn the following useful phrases:

A duì shēntǐ (bù) hǎo.	*A is (not) good for the health/body.*
Y duì X (bù) hǎo.	*Y is (not) good to X.*

Thus **Chōu yān duì wǒde shēntǐ bù hǎo** means *Smoking is not good for my health*.

5 CONJUNCTION: AFTER . . .

In English, you say *after I've been to the restaurant* but in Chinese, you say *I've been to the restaurant after* – the reverse of the English word order:

jiè jiǔ yǐhòu	*after giving up alcohol*
chī fàn yǐhòu	*after eating*

The same happens with **yǐqián** (*before*) and **de shíhou** (*when*).

jiè jiǔ yǐqián	*before giving up alcohol*
fù qián yǐqián	*before paying*
jié zhàng de shíhou	*when working out the bill*

6 RESULTATIVE VERBS: TO EAT YOUR FILL

To say that *you are full* or *you have eaten your fill* in Chinese you put **bǎo** (*full*) after the verb **chī** (*to eat*):

Wǒ chī-bǎo le.	*I'm full* (lit. *I eat full* **le**).

The **le** after the verb shows a completed action (see Unit 4).

To make the verb negative, use **méi** not **bù** and drop the **le** as the verb is then no longer completed.

Other little words, or endings, which appear after the verb in this way have other meanings:

Nǐmen chī-hǎo le ma?	*Have you finished eating (to your satisfaction)?*
Chī-hǎo le.	*Yes, we have (finished eating to our satisfaction).*

Nǐ suàn-cuò le ba.	*You must have got it wrong* (lit. *you calculate wrong* **le***, haven't you*).
Méi suàn-cuò.	*No, I haven't* (lit. *not have calculate wrong*).
Nǐmen hē-wán le ma?	*Have you finished your drinks* (lit. *you drink finish* **le ma**)?
Wǒmen hē-wán le.	*Yes, we have* (lit. *we drink finish* **le**).
Nǐ kàn-jiàn tāmen le ma?	*Did you see them* (lit. *you look perceive them* **le ma**)?
Wǒ méi kàn-jiàn tāmen.	*I didn't see them* (lit. *I not have look perceive them*).

If you put **bù** between the verb and one of these endings as in the examples below, you have the meaning of *cannot* + verb + ending:

Wǒ kàn-bu-jiàn.	*I can't see.*
Tā tīng-bu-dǒng.	*She can't understand* (lit. *she listen cannot understand*).
Wǒmen hē-bu-wán.	*We can't finish (our drinks).*

If on the other hand you put **de** (yes, **de** again!) between the verb and one of these endings, you have the meaning of *can* + verb + ending:

Wǒ kàn-de-jiàn.	*I can see.*
Tāmen tīng-de-dǒng.	*They can understand* (lit. *they listen can understand*).
Wǒmen hē-de-wán.	*We can drink up.*

This is the same **de** as the one used in Unit 8.

7 MEASURE WORDS: CANS, BOWLS AND BOTTLES

You should be familiar with measure words by now, but did you spot the ones for *bottle*, *bowl* and *can* in this unit?

yì píng Fǎguó jiǔ	*a bottle of French wine*
liǎng wǎn(r) chǎomiàn	*two bowls of fried noodles*
liǎng tīng kě(kǒukě)lè	*two cans of cola*

8 DON'T . . . !

To tell somebody not to do something, all you have to do is put the word **bié** (*don't*) in front of what you don't want them to do:

Bié shuō huà.	*Don't speak.*
Bié zǒu.	*Don't go.*

Adding **le** at the end of such sentences helps to soften the idea of giving an order or command.

Practice

Listening

1 10.09 Listen to the dialogue and tick on the menu what Mr Jones has ordered for his meal. You will need to know the word for *beer*, which is **píjiǔ** in Chinese.

Fúwùyuán	Nín xiǎng chī diǎnr shénme?
Mr Jones	Wǒ xǐhuan chī là de.
Fúwùyuán	Wǒmen yǒu yúxiāng ròusī hé mápó dòufu.
Mr Jones	Wǒ yào yí ge yúxiāng ròusī ba.
Fúwùyuán	Nín yào tāng ma?
Mr Jones	Nǐmen yǒu shénme tāng?
Fúwùyuán	Suānlà tāng hé zhàcài tāng.
Mr Jones	Lái yí ge suānlà tāng ba.
Fúwùyuán	Yào jiǔ ma?
Mr Jones	Yào yì píng píjiǔ.
Fúwùyuán	Wǔxīng píjiǔ háishi Qīngdǎo píjiǔ?
Mr Jones	Lái yì píng Wǔxīng píjiǔ.
Fúwùyuán	Hǎo de.

2 How many? Put the correct number and measure word under each of the items in the following pictures. You may not be able to use all of these measure words: **píng, bāo, gè, bēi, zhāng, wǎn, jiàn, tīng, zhī**.

Example: **yì běn shū** (*a book*)

3 Have things changed? If something has changed, you use . . . **le**. If it has not changed, you say **méi yǒu**, or **gēn yǐqián yíyàng** (*the same as before*).

Example: Dōngxi guì le ma?
Guì le (yìdiǎnr).
Méi yǒu / Gēn yǐqián yíyàng.

a Dōngxi guì le ma? (compared with five years ago)
b Nǐ pàng le ma? (compared with five years ago)
c Tiānqi lěng le ma? (compared with a month ago)
d Nǐ zhǎng (*to grow*) gāo le ma? (compared with five years ago)

10 Nín xiǎng chī shénme?

4 The following dialogue is between you and a server. Complete your part.

a	You	(*Server! The bill please.*)
	Fúwùyuán	Nǐmen chī-hǎo le ma?
b	You	(*Yes. Thank you.*)
	Fúwùyuán	Yígòng sānbǎi kuài.
c	You	(*I think you've got it wrong.*)
	Fúwùyuán	Wǒ zài kànkan (*let me look at it again*). Duìbuqǐ. Wǒ suàn-cuò le.
d	You	(*That's all right.*)

5 Which is correct, **méi** or **bù**, in the following sentences?

   a Tā yǐqián chōu yān, xiànzài méi/bù chōu yān le.
   b Wǒ liùyuè qù dù jià le, xiànzài méi/bù yǒu jià le.
   c Yǐqián wǒ yǒu yì tiáo gǒu (*dog*), xiànzài méi/bù yǒu le.
   d Tiānqi tài rè le, wǒ méi/bù chī là de le.

Test yourself

1 **10.10** **How would you do the following?**

   a Say that you have already had enough to eat.
   b Ask your Chinese guest to eat/drink a little more.
   c Say the weather is getting hot/cold now.
   d Say (in two different ways) that you are a vegetarian?
   e Say drinking a little wine is good for your health.

2 **Vocabulary and pronunciation**

   a What does the word **shēntǐ** mean?
   b What's the measure word for cans of drink? Is it a) **tǐng** or b) **tīng** or c) **tíng**?
   c Which word means *cash*? Is it a) **xiànzài** or b) **xiànjīn**?
   d Put the tonemarks on **yigong**. What does it mean?
   e You want to say *The bill please*. Do you say a) **Qǐng jié zhàng** or b) **Qǐng jiè yān**?

SELF CHECK

I CAN...
...order a meal and drinks.
...pay the bill.
...say I have given up something.
...handle more verb endings.
...use more measure words.

 KEY CHARACTERS

(**tíng**)
No stopping

Jìnzhǐ tíng chē
No parking (*lit.* forbid stop vehicle)

Here are two more 'warning' signs. You will see signs like these in China. Can you see that one of the four characters on the right hand sign is the same as the one on the left? What do you think the meaning of that character is?

That character is 停 (**tíng**) meaning *to stop*. The other two 'words' are 禁止 (**jìnzhǐ**) meaning *to forbid* which you met in the last unit and 车 (**chē**) which means *vehicle*.

10 Nín xiǎng chī shénme?

Review 2

Before you tackle the Final review let's do some revision exercises that relate more specifically to Units 6–9.

We'll start with Unit 6

1 **Tomorrow evening it is your turn to entertain your business colleagues from China.**
   a You don't know whether to take them to a concert or to a musical (**yīnyuèjù**) so what do you ask them?
   b They want to go to a concert. How do you ask them whether they like Western music?
   c They assure you that they want to listen to Western music so what do they say to you?

Now for Unit 7

2 **The following passage is about a sweater. Turn all the statements into the negative or into the opposite of what is stated in the sentence.**

Wǒ xǐhuan zhè jiàn máoyī. Zhè jiàn máoyī shìhé wǒ. Zhè jiàn máoyī bú guì. Zhǐyào yìbǎi wǔshí kuài.

Now for Unit 8

3 **Refer back to Dialogue 1 in Unit 8 and answer the following questions in Chinese.**
   a How much was the sweater?
   b What could Eli have bought for the money instead?

4 **Answer the following questions in Chinese.**
   a Somebody asks you whether French goods are more expensive than British ones. What do you reply?
   b The same person compliments you on your spoken Chinese. What is your response?

Now for Unit 9

5 **You need to tell a Chinese friend your itinerary once you have left home so they can book your hotel in Beijing and arrange your programme.**

146

a Tell them that you are going by air to Hong Kong first and staying there two days.
   b Then you are going from Hong Kong to Shanghai by train.
   c You plan to travel by air to Beijing on the morning of 10 August.
6 **The same friend asks if you have ever been to Shanghai. What do they say to you?**

Final review

1 10.11 **On the audio, you will hear different years being said. Repeat each one and write it down.**

Example: yī-jiǔ-jiǔ-qī nián 1997

2 **You have learnt two ways of asking yes or no questions. Can you try to turn the following statements into questions using both ways?**

Example: Statement – **Jīntiān tiānqi hěn hǎo.**
            Question 1 – **Jīntiān tiānqi hǎo ma?**
            Question 2 – **Jīntiān tiānqi hǎo bu hǎo?**

   a Tāmen shì jiěmèi.
   b Tāde chǎomiàn zhēn hǎochī.
   c Míngtiān tā tàitai qù mǎi dōngxi.
   d Nǐ bú rènshi tā.
   e Xiǎo Lǐ yǒu yì tiáo hóng kùzi.

3 **Which of the following statements talk about habitual things one does or does not do (call these X), and which state things one has done at some point or has never done (call these Y)?**
   a Xiǎo Fāng chōu-guo yān.
   b Tā měi tiān chōu yān.
   c Tā méi chī-guo Yìdàlì fàn.
   d Tā bù xǐhuan chī Yìdàlì fàn.

4 **Pair up the question words in Chinese with their English equivalents.**

   a **shéi**   1 where
   b **nǎr**   2 what
   c **shénme**   3 which
   d **zěnme**   4 how many
   e **nǎ**   5 who
   f **jǐ**   6 how

5 10.12 **Can you answer the following questions about Samira in Chinese?**

Samira went to the USA in 2006. She studied German for one year in 2012 and visited France in 2019. In 2018, she had Vietnamese food for the first time, and she stopped smoking in 2007. She will visit China and Japan for the first time next year.

    a Tā qù-guo Zhōngguó ma?
    b Tā 2006 nián qù nǎr le?
    c Tā huì shuō Déyǔ ma?
    d Tā qù-guo Fǎguó ma?
    e Tā xiànzài hái chōu yān ma?
    f Tā chī-guo Yuènán fàn ma?
    g Tā míngnián qù nǎr?

10.13

We hope you have enjoyed *Beginners' Mandarin Chinese*. You are now able to communicate in basic Chinese and ask and understand the answers to simple questions. If you have enjoyed this book, why don't you go on to *Complete Chinese* where you will be able to revise what you have learnt in this course and go on to master more complex language?
If you are interested in learning more about Chinese characters why not learn more about this fascinating written language in *Read and Write Chinese Script*?

Answer key

Wǒmen kànkan Hànzì ba! Let's look at Chinese characters!

1 **a** 2, **b** 6, **c** 10, **d** 5, **e** 11, **f** 24, **g** 83, **h** 69, **i** 57, **j** 36.

2 **a** 三 **b** 八 **c** 十 **d** 十五 **e** 四十二 **f** 九十八 **g** 六十七

3 **a** 天, **b** 三, **c** 六, **d** 四

4 **a** 天/日, **b** 期, **c** 期, **d** 星, **e** 星

5 **a** 3 November, **b** 16 June, **c** 11 July, **d** 14 October, **e** 29 August

6 **a** 十二月二十五日 **b** 三月八日

7 **a** 2008, **b** 1937, **c** 1949, **d** 1885, **e** 1642

8 **a** 9.15, **b** 12.25, **c** 6.30, **d** 3.50, **e** 7:45

9 **a** 六点二十分, **b** 差一刻十二点, (十一点三刻, 十二点差一刻) **c** 十点十分, **d** 四点四十八分, **e** 七点半.

UNIT 1

Discovery question

The square box is the pictogram of 'mouth'. Characters such as *to eat, sing, shout*, etc. all have the 'mouth' component, commonly called the radical.

Vocabulary builder

Nǐmen hǎo!	Hello (pl.)
tāmen	they/them
xièxie nǐ	Thank you (sing.)
xièxie nǐmen	Thank you (pl.)

b Nǐmen hǎo!

Dialogue 1

1 Nǐ tàitai hǎo ma? means *How is your wife?*

2 **a** Mr Green. **b** Mrs Green. **c** There are two people, Mr and Mrs Green, hence the plural term nǐmen is used. **d** Xiǎo Wáng's wife is fine.

Dialogue 2

1 Did you notice whether they said the name first and then *thank you*, or the other way round? Yes, it doesn't matter. While Mr Green started with Xiǎo Wáng and then said *thank you*, Mrs Green started with *thank you* and then said Xiǎo Wáng.

2 a xièxie nǐmen **b** Bú yòng xiè

Dialogue 3

1 Please come in; Please sit down.

2 a 3, **b** 2, **c** 1

3 Nǐ tàitai hǎo ma?

4 Nǐ xiānsheng hǎo ma?

Dialogue 4

1 Míngtiān jiàn.

2 No, he didn't. The teacher is not in.

3 Tomorrow.

4 The passage doesn't say.

5 *Ma* is a question particle. Hǎo means *good* or *well*.

Practice

1 a xiānsheng, tàitai
  b Hǎo
  c Hǎo ma?
  d wǒ, nǐ, tā, tā
  e wǒmen, nǐmen, tāmen, tāmen

2 a Nǐ hǎo! **b** Xièxie. **c** Bú yòng xiè.

3 a Nǐ hǎo! **b** Bú yòng xiè. **c** Xièxie. **d** Zàijiàn!

4 a Nǐ hǎo! **b** Lǐ tàitai hǎo ma? **c** Lǐ xiānsheng zài ma? **d** Xièxie (nǐ).

5 a Xièxie. **b** Bú yòng xiè. **c** Zàijiàn. **d** Míngtiān jiàn. **e** Qǐng jìn.
  f Qǐng zuò. **g** Wǒ/Tā hěn hǎo. **h** Nǐ/Tā hǎo ma?

6 a 4, **b** 3, **c** 2, **d** 1

7 b, d, e

Test yourself

1 a Lǐ xiānsheng, nǐ hǎo! or Nǐ hǎo, Lǐ xiānsheng! **b** Nǐ tàitai hǎo ma?
  c Duìbuqǐ. **d** Xièxie nǐ. **e** Bú yòng xiè **f** Zàijiàn

2 a 3rd **b** lǎoshī **c** míngtiān **d** jiàn

UNIT 2

Discovery question

1 b nín

2 a nǐmen; because there are two of them you have to use the plural form.

3 a usually nǐ, especially when the receptionist is young, but use nín if the receptionist is much older than you.

Vocabulary builder

Nǐ jiào shénme míngzi?	*What's your name?*
Nǐ shì shéi?	*Who are you?*
Tā shì shéi?	*Who is he/she?*

1 Nǐ jiào shénme míngzi? Nín guì xìng?

2 a Nǐ shì shéi?

Dialogue 1

1 Pàn Pan is Mrs Li's child.

2 a Three (Jane Lord, Mrs Chen and Pàn Pan).
   b Lord, Chen, and Li (Pàn Pan).
   c No, she doesn't. (She says Wǒ méi yǒu háizi which means I don't have children)

Dialogue 2

1 The Chinese have their surname first.

2 a Cháng

3 b He speaks a little.

Dialogue 3

1 b Wǒ jiào Bái Bǐdé.

2 b Tā zhēn piàoliang.

3 a Zhè shì wǒde péngyou.

4 a Nǐ rènshi bu rènshi tā?

Practice 1

1 Nín guì **xìng**?

2 Nǐ huì bu **huì** shuō Yīngwén?

3 Tā **jiào** Liú Wénguāng.

4 Wǒ **méi** yǒu háizi.

Answer key   151

Language discovery

1   a Yǒu / Méi yǒu (háizi).
    b Yǒu / Méi yǒu (péngyou).
    c Yǒu / Méi yǒu (Zhōngwén míngzi).

2   a Nǐ yǒu méi yǒu háizi?
    b Nǐ rènshi bú rènshi tā?
    c Tā hǎo bù hǎo?
    d Nǐmen shuō bù shuō Zhōngwén?

3   a Tā jiào **shénme** míngzi?
    b Nǐ rènshi **shúi**?
    c Tāmen yǒu **shénme**?

Practice 2

1   a Tā jiào **shénme** míngzi? Tā **jiào** Fāng Yuán.
    b Nǐ huì shuō Zhōngwén ma? Huì. Wǒ huì **shuō** yìdiǎnr.
    c Tāde nán péngyou **shì** shéi? Wǒ bú **rènshi** tā.

2   a Tāmen shì Lǐ xiānsheng、Yīng tàitai. b Tā jiào Lǐ Jīnshēng.
    c Duì. Tā xìng Yīng. d Bù. Tā xìng Lǐ. e Wǒ (bú) rènshi tāmen.

3   a Wáng. b Lányīng. c A little bit. d Chinese teacher.
    e No, she doesn't. f She's quite young. g Yes.

4   a Tā jiào Zhào Huá. Tā shì jǐngchá. b Zhè shì Liú Guāng. Tā shì sījī.
    c Nà shì Guō Jié. Tā shì dàifu. d Tā jiào Lǐ Mínglì. Tā shì lǎoshī.
    e Zhè shì Zhōu Jiābǎo. Tā shì xuésheng. f Nà shì Wú Zébì. Tā shì chúshī.

5   a bú duì, b bú duì, c bú duì, d bú duì, e bú duì, f duì.

6   a Nǐ huì shuō Yīngwén ma? Nǐ huì bu huì shuō Yīngwén?
    b Nǐmen shì lǎoshī ma? Nǐmen shì bu shì lǎoshī?
    c Xiǎo Zhèng zài ma? Xiǎo Zhèng zài bu zài?
    d Lǐ xiānsheng jīntiān lái ma? Lǐ xiānsheng jīntiān lái bu lái?
    e Wáng Fāng yǒu Yīngwén míngzi ma? Wáng Fāng yǒu mei yǒu Yīngwén míngzi?
    f Lín lǎoshī jiào Lín Péng ma? Lín lǎoshī jiào bu jiào Lín Péng?

Test yourself

1 a Nín guì xìng? Nǐ xìng shénme?
  b Wǒ jiào xxx.
  c Wǒ méi yǒu Zhōngwén míngzi.
  d Wǒ bú rènshi tā.
  e Méi guānxi.
  f Wǒde péngyou bú shì lǎoshī.

2 a dāngrán
  b shuō
  c shéi
  d wén

UNIT 3

Discovery question

1 Nǐ/Nín hǎo. Wǒ jiào X. Nǐ jiào shénme? or Nín guì xìng?
2 Nínde/Nǐde diànhuà hàomǎ shì duōshao?

Vocabulary builder

1 Londoner
2 British / British person
3 Chinese / Chinese person

Dialogue 1

1 Zhè shì wǒde míngpiàn.
2 You are Chinese, aren't you?
3 Nín shì Zhōngguó-rén ma? is a neutral question i.e. the speaker asks the question without any supposition whereas Nín shì Zhōngguó-rén ba? would suggest that the speaker assumes the other person is Chinese, but they are not sure about it and want to confirm this supposition.

Dialogue 2

1 Hépíng Fàndiàn.
2 The meaning of the name of the hotel is *peace*.
3 Fēijī piào is *plane ticket*.
4 Yìsi means *meaning*.

Answer key   153

Dialogue 3

1 508.

2 a Píng'ān Lù zài Xīchéng Qū. **b** Hépíng Fàndiàn zài Dōngchéng Qū.

3 Xī and dōng mean *west* and *east* respectively.

4 Hǎo means *good* while hào means *number*.

5 Mr Lin's phone number is 6552 9324. Mr White's phone number is 6673 8830.

Practice

3 a shì/bú shì, **b** shì/bú shì, **c** shì/bú shì, **d** shì/bú shì, **e** shì/bù zhīdào, **f** shì/bù zhīdào.

4 Speaker 1: Nǐ hǎo! Wǒ jiào Chén Lìmǐn. Wǒ shì Xiānggǎng-rén. Wǒ zhù zài Xiānggǎng Lì Yè Lù 8 hào. Wǒde diànhuà hàomǎ shì 507 1293.

Speaker 2: Nǐ hǎo! Wǒ jiào Wú Yīfēi. Wǒ shì Shànghǎi-rén. Wǒde diànhuà hàomǎ shì 874 3659. Wǒ zhù zài Shànghǎi Nánjīng Lù 9 hào.

Speaker 3: Wǒ jiào Guō Wànjí. Wǒ shì Fǎguó-rén. Wǒ zhù zài Běijīng Hépíng Lù 6 hào. Wǒde diànhuà hàomǎ shì 724 6274.

6 a Běijīng Cháoyáng Lù èr hào, Lǐ Mínglì lǎoshī. **b** Sūzhōu Lónghǎi Lù jiǔ hào, Dōngfāng Fàndiàn sān-bā-sì fángjiān, Zhào Huá xiānsheng. **c** Nánjīng Xīchéng Qū Hépíng Lù wǔ hào, Zhào Jiābǎo xiǎojie.

7 a 3, **b** 7, **c** 1, **d** 5, **e** 2, **f** 4, **g** 6.

Test yourself

1 a Tā shì shéi?
  b Nǐ zhù (zài) nǎr?
  c Wǒ bú zhù (zài) Lúndūn.
  d Nǐde diànhuà hàomǎ shì duōshao?
  e Diànhuà shì shénme yìsi?
  f Zhè shì wǒde fēijī piào.

2 a hào
  b Lúndūn
  c guó
  d meaning

UNIT 4

Discovery question

1 a Have you eaten?

2 True.

3 shíwǔ and wǔshí

Vocabulary builder

1 a 5, **b** 2, **c** 1, **d** 3, **e** 4

2 a 3, **b** 4, **c** 1, **d** 5, **e** 2

Dialogue 1

1 Yǒu mei yǒu háizi?

2 Mr Liu has two children.

3 They are two (the son) and five (the daughter).

Dialogue 2

1 Liú Fúguì has two brothers and one sister.

2 The two brothers are 26 and 24 respectively. His sister is 28.

Dialogue 3

1 Wú says that Lù's parents don't look their age. He also says that Lù's sister is very young.

2 a Lù xiānsheng de bàba wǔshísān.
b Lù xiānsheng de māma sìshíjiǔ.
c Lù xiānsheng de mèimei jīnnián èrshí'èr.
d Lù xiānsheng de mèimei méi yǒu jié hūn.
e Lù xiānsheng de mèimei yǒu nán péngyou le.

Language discovery

1 a He/she is coming. **b** He/she has come.

2 a běn, **b** zhāng, **c** zhāng

3 a èr, **b** liǎng

4 Both a and b are appropriate responses to *thank you*.

Practice

1 a èrshíjiǔ, **b** qīshíyī, **c** sānshí'èr

2 a èrshíyī, **b** qīshí, **c** liùshíliù, **d** sìshíjiǔ, **e** sānshí, **f** liùshí, **g** shíwǔ, **h** sānshísān

Answer key   155

3 Dīng Fèng is married. She has two children, a son and a daughter. Her son is called Dīng Míng and is 12 this year. Her daughter's name is Dīng Yīng. She is 14 years old.

4 a Méi yǒu. **b** Méi yǒu. **c** Bú shì. (Tā bú shì lǎoshī.) **d** Wǒ méi yǒu háizi. **e** Wǒ méi yǒu dìdi.

5 a Are you married? = 4, **b** How old is she? = 3, **c** What's Mr Wang, the teacher, called? = 1, **d** Have you any children? = 5, **e** Has Mrs Li a daughter? = 2

6 a He is 20. **b** He has one brother and one sister. **c** Both of them are younger than him. **d** They are 15 and 17 respectively. **e** They are both students.

7 Wǒ jiào Mǎlì, jīnnián shíqī suì. Wǒ méi yǒu jiějie, méi yǒu mèimei. Wǒ yǒu yí ge gēge, yí ge dìdi. Wǒ gēge jiào Hēnglì. Tā èrshí suì. Wǒ dìdi jiào Bǐdé. Tā shíwǔ suì. Wǒmen dōu shì xuésheng.

Test yourself

1 a Nǐ hǎo! **b** Nǐ jiào shénme? **c** Nǐ jǐ suì? **d** Nǐ yǒu xiōngdì、jiěmèi ma? **e** Xièxie (nǐ). **f** Zàijiàn!

2 a liǎng, **b** xiǎo, **c** gēge, **d** hé

UNIT 5

Discovery question

1 Either would be fine, but most people would probably use nǐ.

2 You would normally use nín as he/she is likely to be 'senior' in position in their company.

3 Normally nín for teachers regardless of their age. However, these days, young or younger teachers tend to accept nǐ more readily.

Vocabulary builder

1 a 5, **b** 1, **c** 4, **d** 2, **e** 3

2 a 4, **b** 1, **c** 2, **d** 3, **e** 5

3 a 1, **b** 3, **c** 4, **d** 2

4 a 2, **b** 3, **c** 1

Dialogue 1

They're every day from 8 a.m. to 5.30 p.m.

Dialogue 2

1 He thought he had missed the beginning of the meeting.

2 It was Wednesday. Xiǎo Xú thought it was Thursday.

NEW EXPRESSIONS

a bāng = help **b** bàn = half

Dialogue 3

Mǎ Tè 's train has been cancelled and he doesn't know what to do.

She helped him find the time of the next train and which platform it was leaving from.

Dialogue 4

So does Ann's birthday fall on Chinese New Year? Well, not if she uses GMT in the UK but it does if she uses Beijing time in China. i.e. the time in China (Beijing) is eight hours later than GMT.

Practice

2 a yīyuè yī hào, **b** shí'èryuè èrshíwǔ hào, **c** sānyuè bā hào, **d** shíyuè yī hào

3 a 9 September **b** Sunday morning **c** Thursday, 28 November **d** 10.45 a.m. Saturday **e** 3.30 p.m. Friday, 6 July **f** 11 a.m. Monday, 31 December.

5 a Wǔ diǎn yí kè; wǔ diǎn shíwǔ fēn. **b** Chà wǔ fēn wǔ diǎn; sì diǎn wǔshíwǔ fēn. **c** (Hái yǒu) sìshí fēnzhōng. **d** Zǎoshang wǔ diàn líng wǔ fēn. **e** Wǔ diǎn líng qī fēn.

Test yourself

1 a Sānyuè sānshí hào.
  b Xīngqīsì.
  c Sì diǎn èrshíqī fēn.
  d Sì diǎn sān kè or chà yí kè wǔ diǎn. Dì-sān zhàntái.
  e Sì diǎn wǔshí fēn or Wǔ diǎn chà shí fēn. Dì-yī zhàntái.

2 a dōu
  b shàngwǔ
  c three weeks
  d sānyuè is March while sān ge yuè means 'three months'
  e 'zhīdao' means to know

Key characters

Yes, they would be 上 and 下.

REVIEW 1

1 a Qǐng jìn. **b** Nǐ hǎo. **c** Qǐng zuò. **d** Míngtiān jiàn.

5 a Nǐ zhù zài shénme fàndiàn? (Nǐ zhù zài) jǐ hào fángjiān?
b Zhè shì wǒde míngpiàn.

6 a Chén xiānsheng, nǐ hǎo ma? Nǐ jiào shénme míngzi? Nǐ huì bu huì shuō Yīngwén? Nǐ zhù zài nǎr? Nǐ jié hūn le ma? Nǐ yǒu háizi ma? Nǐ(de) háizi jǐ suì/duō dà? Nǐde diànhuà hàomǎ shì duōshao/shénme? Nǐ rènshi bu rènshi X? Nǐ shì Běijīng-/Shànghǎi-/Guǎngdōng-rén ma? Nǐ bàba\māma dōu zài (Běijīng) ma?

7 liùshísì, èrshíjiǔ, wǔshíqī, sānshíbā, shí'èr, jiǔshíwǔ, sìshí, èr, qīshísān, shí.

8 a Wǒ yào xīngqīsì shàngwǔ jiǔ diǎn bàn de huǒchē piào.

9 a yī-jiǔ-jiǔ-qī nián yīyuè liù hào **b** èr-líng-líng-líng nián sānyuè èrshíyī hào **c** yī-jiǔ-sì-sān nián bāyuè shíwǔ hào

UNIT 6

Discovery question

People normally say dǎ tàijí but zuò qìgōng. If you remember that tàijí is known as a form of shadow boxing, you would appreciate why dǎ (*to hit*) is the verb (or action) that goes with it.

Vocabulary builder

1 a 2, **b** 1, **c** 4, **d** 3

2 a Niújīn gēn Jiànqiáo yíyàng, dōu hěn yǒumíng (famous).
b Yīngguó yīngwén gēn Měiguó yīngwén bù yíyàng.
c A bǐ B dà.
d B bǐ A hǎo.

Dialogue 1

Shàngwǔ: to go to the bank (qù yínháng) and exchange money (huàn qián) (first), and (then) go shopping (lit. go to shops) (qù shāngdiàn) and buy things (mǎi dōngxi)

Xiàwǔ: to go to Beihai Park (qù Běihǎi Gōngyuán)

Wǎnshang: to watch acrobatics (kàn zájì)

Dialogue 2

1 They have considered the options of watching a movie (kàn diànyǐng) or going to a Peking Opera (kàn jīngjù).

2 They finally decided to go to a concert (tīng yīnyuèhuì).

3 a with a problem/problematic; no problem **b** interesting; uninteresting **c** same; different **d** difficult; easy

4 a nán **b** méi yìsi **c** yíyàng

Dialogue 3

Frank saw people doing Tai Chi (dǎ tàijíquán) and qigong (zuò qìgōng). (Please note the different verbs (dǎ vs zuò) for the two forms of exercise.)

Practice

1 a Tā zài mǎi dōngxi. **b** Tāmen zài kàn zájì. **c** Tā zài huàn qián. **d** Tā zài dǎ tàijíquán. **e** Tāmen zài kàn diànyǐng. **f** Tā zài tīng yīnyuè.

3 a bù yíyàng (gāo), **b** yíyàng (dà), **c** bù yíyàng (zhòng), **d** bù yíyàng (gāo), **e** yíyàng (zhòng), **f** bù yíyàng (dà).

4 a Bú duì. Xǔ bǐ Hú gāo. **b** Bú duì. Hú bǐ Qū zhòng. **c** Bú duì. Tāmen yíyàng dà. **d** Duì. **e** Duì.

5 a Xīngqītiān, **b** xīngqīsì xiàwǔ, **c** xīngqīsān wǎnshang, **d** shàngwǔ, **e** xīngqīliù.

Test yourself

1 a Nǐ míngtiān xiǎng zuò shénme?
 b Xiǎo Mǎ gēn tā jiějie yíyàng gāo.
 c Wǒ juéde zájì bǐ jīngjù yǒu yìsi.
 d Xiǎo Zhào, jīntiān wǎnshang nǐ xiǎng qù nǎr?
 e Lǐ xiǎojie, nǐ xiǎng qù kàn diànyǐng háishi tīng yīnyuèhuì?

2 a gēn **b** in question forms **c** yǒu wèntí **d** nán **e** yīnyuè

Key characters.

男 means 'male'. 女 means 'female'.

The character 女 means 'woman'. 男 means 'man'.

UNIT 7

Discovery question

Fā means *to expand* or *prosperous*. The phrase literally means *congratulations (on) expanding wealth* (cái). That is why people like the number 8 (bā) which sounds close to fā.

Vocabulary builder

a liùbǎi **b** liùbǎi yīshí **c** sìbǎi jiǔshíqī **d** sìbǎi líng èr **e** qīqiān

Dialogue 1

2 **a** X gěi wǒ kànkan xíng ma? **b** X wǒ shìshi kěyǐ ma?

3 **a** X hěn hǎo. **b** X búcuò. **c** X (hěn) shìhé nǐ.

Dialogue 2

a Well, it is neither far nor near. It's two bus stops away.

b They could walk (zǒu lù) or take the bus (zuò chē).

c They decided to go there by bus (zuò chē).

Dialogue 3

2 **a** My apples are a little bigger than theirs.
   b My grapes are much sweeter than theirs.
   c My strawberries are much fresher than theirs.

3 **a** mǎi **b** nà **c** yuǎn

Language discovery

1 **a** wèi **b** jiàn **c** běn **d** píng

2 **a** wǔ máo èr (fēn), **b** liǎng/èr kuài liǎng/èr máo wǔ, **c** shí'èr kuài qī máo liù, **d** jiǔshíjiǔ kuài jiǔ máo jiǔ, **e** èr/liǎngbǎi líng wǔ kuài wǔ máo sì. **f** bā kuài líng qī (fēn).

3 **a** Nà ge shìchǎng yuǎn ma? or Nà ge shìchǎng yuǎn bu yuǎn?
   b Nà ge shìchǎng lí zhèlǐ duō yuǎn?
   c Běijīng lí Tiānjīn yǒu yìbǎi gōnglǐ ma?

4 **a** liù、qī kuài
   b shí qī、bā jīn
   c sānshísì、wǔ tiān

5 **a** Pútao bǐ píngguǒ guì (yìdiǎnr).
   b Xiǎo Wáng bǐ Lǎo Lǐ gāo yìdiǎnr.
   c Běijīng bǐ Lúndūn rè duōle.
   d Bái xiānsheng bǐ Bái tàitai dà deduō.

6 **a** jiù, **b** jiù, **c** cái, **d** jiù, **e** cái.

Practice

1 a wǔ máo èr (fēn), **b** liǎng/èr kuài liǎng/èr máo wǔ, **c** shí'èr kuài qī máo liù, **d** jiǔshíjiǔ kuài jiǔ máo jiǔ, **e** èr/liǎngbǎi líng wǔ kuài wǔ máo sì. **f** bā kuài líng qī (fēn).

2 a Píngguǒ jiǔshí biànshì yì jīn. **b** Pútao yí bàng sì-jiǔ yì jīn. **c** Cǎoméi yí bàng qī-wǔ yì hé. **d** Xiāngjiāo jiǔshíjiǔ biànshì yì jīn.

3 a Xīhóngshì zěnme mài? **b** Báicài yì jīn duōshao qián? **c** Tǔdòu duōshao qián yì jīn?

4 a Yú zěnme mài? Qī kuài líng jiǔ yì jīn. **b** Cǎoméi duōshao qián yì hé? Qī kuài sì yì hé. **c** Báicài yì jīn duōshao qián? Yí kuài èr yì jīn. **d** Pútao guì bu guì? Bú guì. Yí kuài jiǔ yì jīn. **e** Wǒ mǎi liǎng jīn tǔdòu. Sān kuài èr.

5 a Tài dà le! **b** Tài rè le! **c** Tāde qián tài duōle! **d** (Piào) tài guì le! **e** Fǎwén tài nán le!

Test yourself

1 a Zhǐ yào wǔ fēnzhōng jiù dào.
b Yào/děi wǔshí fēnzhōng cái dào.
c Zài wǒ jiā wǒ bàba zuì dà.
d Diànyǐngyuàn lí wǒ jiā bù yuǎn.
e Xiāngjiāo sìshíjiǔ biànshì yí bàng.

2 a jīn: half a kilogram; jìn: near, close
b mǎi: to buy; mài: to sell
c jiàn (as for a sweater)
d bǎi
e shìshi

UNIT 8

Discovery question

1 Either Guòjiǎng, guòjiǎng, Nǎli, nǎli, hái xíng or còuhe. Of course, it is perfectly OK for you to say xièxie.

2 They are saying *My English is really not that good*.

Vocabulary builder

1 hǎo / good; **2** hái kěyǐ / just so so; **3** búcuò / not bad, pretty good; **4** bù zěnmeyàng / not so good; **5** fēicháng hǎo / extremely good or excellent; **6** bù hǎo / not good or bad; **7** hěn bù hǎo / very bad; **8** fēicháng bù hǎo / extremely bad or terrible.

Dialogue 1

He started by saying búcuò, búcuò (not bad/quite nice). He then said it was yǒu diǎnr dà (*a little too big*). As for the color he said bù nánkàn (*not 'bad-looking'*). When he heard the price (yìbǎi wǔshí kuài, i.e. 150 yuan, he was 'shocked' and said shénme?! (*What?!*) He finally said Yìbǎi wǔshí kuài wǒ kěyǐ mǎi sān zhāng zúqiú piào (*With 150 kuai, I could have bought three football match tickets*).

Dialogue 2

1 Mr Li went to France and Italy. The dialogue doesn't say where Mrs Law went.

2 Mr Li's holiday was very good though he said things were more expensive in France and Italy than in the UK.

3 Mrs Law's holiday was not that good because it rained every day.

Dialogue 3

Baojie is going to help Martin with his Chinese and Martin is going to help Baojie with her English.

Language discovery

1 a Lǐ xiānsheng Déwén (German) shuō-de fēicháng hǎo. **b** Zhāng tàitai jiàqī guò-de bú tài hǎo. **c** Cháo xiǎojie Yīngwén xué-de kuài-jíle. **d** Mǎlì yòng kuàizi yòng-de bù zěnmeyàng. **e** Hēnglì shuō Rìyǔ shuō-de hěn qīngchu.

2 a gèng hǎo **b** gèng kuài **c** gèng héshì

3 a měi (ge) rén **b** měi ge píngguǒ **c** měi jiàn máoyī **d** měi běn shū

Culture point

At Chinese New Year, adults usually give children a hóng bāo (little red envelope), which contains qián (money).

Practice

1 a 5, **b** 6, **c** 4, **d** 1, **e** 2, **f** 7, **g** 3.

2 a yí jiàn bái chènyī, **b** yí jiàn huáng dàyī, **c** yí tào lán xīfú, **d** yì tiáo lǜ qúnzi, **e** yì shuāng hēi xié, **f** yì tiáo hóng kùzi.

3 a Xiǎo Cài is wearing a white shirt, a blue skirt and a pair of red leather shoes. **b** Xiǎo Zhào is wearing a blue silk shirt, black trousers and green cloth shoes. **c** Lǎo Fāng is wearing a black suit, a white shirt and a pair of black leather shoes.

4 a Lǎo Mǎ chuān yì shuāng hēi píxié、yí jiàn lán chènyī. **b** Xiǎo Qián chuān yí jiàn hóng chènyī、(yì tiáo) hēi kùzi、yì shuāng bùxié. **c** Liú xiānsheng chuān yí tào huī xīfú、huáng chènyī、zōng píxié.

5 a Zhāng Tóng méi yǒu Mǎ Fēng dà. Mǎ Fēng méi yǒu Zhāng Tóng gāo, yě méi yǒu tā niánqīng. **b** Zhāng Tóng de diànnǎo méi yǒu Mǎ Fēng de diànnǎo guì, yě méi yǒu Mǎ Fēng de diànnǎo dà. **c** Mǎ Fēng de zì méi yǒu Zhāng Tóng de zì qīngchu.

Test yourself

1 a Nǐde Yīngwén shuō-de zhēn hǎo.
  b Zhè jiàn chènyī yǒu (yì) diǎnr xiǎo.
  c Nǐde jiàqī guò-de zěnmeyàng?
  d Nírìlìyà bǐ Yīnggélán dà.
  e Mòxīgē méi yǒu Bāxī dà.

2 a dà: big; xiǎo: small **b** guì **c** màn **d** yǔ **e** yǐhòu

UNIT 9

Discovery question

1 xī

2 nán

Vocabulary builder

1 a, **2** b, **3** b

Dialogue 1

1 Xiǎo Fēng is going to Xiānggǎng (*Hong Kong*) and Àomén (*Macao*). She will zuò fēijī qù (*fly to*) Hong Kong first and then zuò chuán qù (*take a boat to*) Macao.

2 Lǎo Qiáo says he is not sure how long his holiday will be because he will be retiring in December.

Dialogue 2

1 To get to Tiāntán (Temple of Heaven), you can take a bus (zuò chē) and it is four stops (sì zhàn). Both Bus No. 15 (shíwǔ lù) and Bus No. 23 (èrshísān lù) will get you there. No need to change (bú yòng huàn chē). When you get off (xià chē), you walk on a little (wǎng qián zǒu yìdiǎnr) and Tiāntán is on the west side of the road (mǎlù xībianr).

2 a southwest
   b Buses number 15 and 23
   c four
   d west side (of the road)
   e wǎng dōng / wǎng xī

Dialogue 3

1 James suggested that they cycle to Tianjin. Huang didn't accept it and thought cycling to Tianjin was both tiring and dangerous.

2 b

3 a

4 b

5 a

Language discovery

1 a Chē yào lái le.
   b Chē jiù/kuài yào lái le.

2 a cóng Yīngguó dào Měiguó
   b cóng jīntiān dào míngtiān
   c cóng jīnnián dào míngnián

3 a Nǐ qù-guò Déguó ma?
   b Nǐ xué-guò Déguó huà / Déwén ma?
   c Nǐ chī-guò Déguó fàn ma?

4 a xiān chī fàn, zài qù mǎi dōngxi
   b xiān qù mǎi dōngxi zài qù kàn diànyǐng
   c xiān xué Zhōngwén zài qù Zhōngguó

5 a Wǒ yào zhù X tiān?
   b Wǒ xué le X ge yuè de Zhōngwén.

6 a Huì qù *or* bú huì qù.
   b Huì qù *or* bú huì qù.

7 a yòu hǎo yòu shūfu
   b yòu bù hǎo yòu guì
   c yòu piányi yòu hǎo

Practice

1 a Qù-guo *or* méi qù-guo.
   b zuò-guo *or* méi zuò-guo
   c kàn-guo *or* méi kàn-guo
   d chī-guo *or* méi chī-guo
   e hē-guo *or* méi hē-guo

2 Recording: First walk southwards. When you get to East Sea Road, take an eastbound bus for two stops and you will find the cinema on the south side of the road opposite the shop. The answer is F.

3 Wǎng xī zǒu, guò liǎng ge lùkǒu, wǎng běi guǎi. Fàndiàn jiù zài lù de dōngbianr.

4 B = school; C = shop; D = Donghai Park; E = Bank of China.

8 a Fǎguó hé Yìdàlì. **b** Sì tiān. **c** Gēn tāde Fǎguó péngyou. Tāmen kāi chē qù. **d** Yí ge xīngqī. **e** Zuò fēijī. **f** Kāi chē.

Recording: Mr White is going on holiday soon. He is going to two places. He'll first go from London to Paris by train. He plans to stay in Paris for four days. After that he and his French friend will drive to Italy. They will stay in Italy for a week. Lastly he will fly back to London from Italy. His friend will drive back to France.

Test yourself

1 a Qù Zhōngguó Yínháng zěnme zǒu?
  b Zuò shí lù (gōnggòng) qìchē.
  c Zuò wǔ zhàn.
  d Wǒde péngyou méi (yǒu) qù-guo Zhōngguó.
  e Kuài (yào) xià yǔ le.

2 a Xiānggǎng
  b nàr
  c Macao
  d from
  e Yes, it's huàn.

UNIT 10

Discovery question

1 c gānbēi

2 a the one facing the door

3 a True (except for some areas in the south).
  b False. (It is appropriate, even common, for the host to do so.)

Dialogue 1

1 a Drinks: white wine, juice
  b Food: beancurd, vegetables (though not explicitly ordered)

2 a yes

3 b Yuqiao

4 a hot

Dialogue 2

1 b Yuqiao
2 d It was a little too late to drink coffee then.
3 c bubble tea
4 a cash only

Dialogue 3

1 b They had some food at a food stall.
2 c The price of the noodles they had has gone up.
3 They had chǎomiàn (*fried noodles*) and kěkǒukělè (which needs no translation).
4 The price of a bowl of chǎomiàn (*noodles*) had increased from èrshí kuài yì wǎnr (*20 kuai per bowl*) to èrshíwǔ kuài (*25 kuai*).

Practice

1 Recording: Mr. Jones ordered yúxiāng ròusī (*fish flavoured shredded meat*), zhàcài tāng (*pickled vegetable soup*) and Wǔxīng píjiǔ (*Fivestar beer*).

2 a yì wǎn chǎomiàn, **b** sì píng pútáojiǔ, **c** liǎng bāo táng,
d wǔ tīng kěkǒukělè, **e** liǎng wǎn tāng, **f** sān zhāng piào.

3 a Guì le *or* Méi yǒu *or* Gēn yǐqián yíyàng.
b Pàng le *or* Méi yǒu *or* Gēn yǐqián yíyàng.
c Lěng le *or* Méi yǒu *or* Gēn yǐqián yíyàng.
d Zhǎng gāo le *or* Méi yǒu *or* Gēn yǐqián yíyàng.

4 a Fúwùyuán, qǐng jié zhàng. **b** Chī-hǎo le. Xièxie. **c** Nǐ suàn-cuò le ba.
d Méi guānxi.

5 a bù, **b** méi, **c** méi, **d** bù.

Test yourself

1 a Wǒ (yǐjīng) chī bǎo le.
b Zài duō chī/hē yìdiǎn(r).
c Tiānqi rè/lěng le.
d Wǒ chī sù./Wǒ bù chī ròu.
e Hē yìdiǎn(r) jiǔ duì shēntǐ hǎo.

2 a body/health
b (b) tīng

  c (b) xiànjīn
  d yígòng (altogether)
  e (a) Qǐng jié zhàng

Review 2

1 a Nǐmen xiǎng tīng yīnyuèjù háishi kàn xì?
  b Nǐmen xǐhuan (tīng) Xīfāng yīnyuè ma? Nǐmen xǐhuan bu xǐhuan (tīng) Xīfāng yīnyuè?
  c Zài Xīfāng dāngrán tīng Xīfāng yīnyuè.

2 Wǒ bù xǐhuan zhè jiàn máoyī. Zhè jiàn máoyī bù shìhé wǒ. Zhè jiàn máoyī hěn guì (or tài guì le). Yìbǎi wǔshí kuài.

3 a Yìbǎi wǔshí kuài. **b** Sān zhāng zúqiú piào.

4 a Fǎguó de dōngxi bǐ Yīngguó de (dōngxi) guì. Fǎguó de dōngxi méi yǒu Yīngguó de (dōngxi) guì. Fǎguó de dōngxi gēn Yīngguó de (dōngxi) yíyàng guì. **b** Nǎli, nǎli, shuō-de bù hǎo. (or Xièxie.)

5 a Wǒ xiān zuò fēijī qù Xiānggǎng. Zài nàr zhù liǎng tiān. **b** Ránhòu (cóng Xiānggǎng) zuò huǒchē qù Shànghǎi. **c** Wǒ dǎsuàn bāyuè shí hào (cóng Shànghǎi) zuò fēijī qù Běijīng.

6 Nǐ qù-guo Shànghǎi ma? Nǐ qù-guo Shànghǎi méi you?

Final review

1 1066, 1462, 1798, 1914, 1945, 2000, 2008.

2 a Tāmen shì bu shì jiěmèi? Tāmen shì jiěmèi ma?
  b Tāde chǎomiàn hǎochī bu hǎochī? Tāde chǎomiàn hǎochī ma?
  c Míngtiān tā tàitai qù bu qù mǎi dōngxi? Míngtiān tā tàitai qù mǎi dōngxi ma?
  d Nǐ rènshi bu rènshi tā? Nǐ bú rènshi tā ma?
  e Xiǎo Lǐ yǒu mei yǒu yì tiáo hóng kùzi? Xiǎo Lǐ yǒu yì tiáo hóng kùzi ma?

3 a Y, **b** X, **c** Y, **d** X.

4 a 5, **b** 1, **c** 2, **d** 6, **e** 3, **f** 4

5 a Méi qù-guo. **b** Qù Měiguó le. **c** Huì shuō. **d** Qù-guo. **e** Bù chōu le. **f** Chī-guo. **g** Qù Zhōngguó hé Rìběn.

Chinese–English vocabulary

The number after each vocabulary item indicates the unit in which it first appears.

Ài'ěrlán   *Ireland*   3
àiren   (sometimes used in the People's Republic) *husband/wife*   10
ānquán   *safe*   9
Àomén   *Macao*   9

ba   (particle indicating suggestion)   3
bàba   *dad, father*   4
bǎi   *hundred*   7
bái(sè) (de)   *white*   7
bàn   *half*   5
bāng   *to help*   5
bēi   *a cup of; cup*   10
běi   *north*   9
bǐ   *compared to*   6
biān   *side*   9
bié   *don't*   9
bīngqílín   *ice cream*   10
bù   *not*   1
bú kèqi   *you are welcome*   4
bú xiàng   *not look (like) it*   4
bú yòng xiè   *not at all* (lit. *no need thank*)   1
bù zěnmeyàng   *not so good*   8
búcuò   *pretty good, not bad*   7

cái   *not ... until, only then*   7
cài   *dish*   10
càidān   *menu*   10
cǎoméi   *strawberry*   7

cèsuǒ   *toilet*   6
chà   *lacking, short of*   5
Chángchéng   *the Great Wall*   10
chǎomiàn   *stir-fried noodles*   10
chē   *vehicle* (bus, bike, car)   6
chēzhàn   *bus stop, train station*   9
chī   *to eat*   10
chī-bǎo le   *to eat one's fill*   10
chī sù   *to be vegetarian*   10
chōu (yān)   *to smoke (a cigarette)*   10
chuán   *ship, boat*   9
Chūnjié   *the Spring Festival, Chinese New Year*   5
chūzū (qì)chē   *taxi*   9
cóng   *from*   9

dà   *big, old*   4
dǎ tàijíquán   *to do Tai Chi*   6
dāngrán   *of course*   2
dào   *to arrive; to go to*   5, 7
dǎsuàn   *to plan*   9
dàxiǎo   *size*   8
de   (possessive indicator)   2
... deduō   *much (more)* ...   7
Déguó   *Germany*   3
dì   (for ordinal numbers)   5
diǎn   *o'clock*   5
diànhuà   *phone*   3
diànnǎo   *computer*   8
diànshì   *television*   9

diànyǐng *film, movie* 6
dìdi *younger brother* 4
dìfang *place* 9
dìng *to book (a ticket)* 6
dōng *east* 9
dōngxi *thing, object* 6
dōu *all; both* 5
dòufu *beancurd, tofu* 10
dù jià *to take a holiday* 9
duì *yes, correct* 3
duì *to; for* 10
duìbuqǐ *excuse me, I'm sorry* 1
duìmiàn *opposite* 9
duō *many, more* 10
duō cháng? *how long?* 7
duō yuǎn? *how far?* 7
duōshao? *how much, how many, what's the number of?* 3

è *hungry* 10
érzi *son* 4
fā fēng *mad* 9
Fǎguó *France* 3
fàndiàn *hotel* 3
fángjiān *room* 3
fǎnzhèng *no way; in any case* 9
fēicháng *extremely* 8
fēijī *plane* 3
fēn(zhōng) *minute* 5
fù qián *pay (money)* 10
fúwùyuán *assistant, housestaff* 6
gè *(measure word)* 4
gēge *elder brother* 4
gěi *for; to give* 6
gēn *and; with; to follow* 6
gèng *even more* 8
gōngjīn *kilogram* 7
guān (mén) *to close (a door)* 5
Guǎngdōng *Canton (Province)* 3
guì *expensive; honorable* 2
guò *to pass, to spend* (time) 8

-guo *have ever done* (verbal suffix) 9

hái *still* 5
hái kěyǐ *just so so* 8
háishi *or* (used in question forms) 6
háishi *would be better* 9
háizi *child* 2
Hànzì *Chinese characters*
hǎo *good, well* 1
hào *number* 3
hǎochī (de) *delicious, tasty* 10
hàomǎ *number* (often used for phone numbers and car registration plates) 3
hē *to drink* 10
hé *and* 4
hēi(sè) (de) *black* 7
hěn *very* 1
hépíng *peace* 3
héshì *suitable* 8
hóng(sè) (de) *red* 7
huàn *to change* 9
huàn qián *to change money* 6
huáng(sè) (de) *yellow* 7
huì *can, be able to* 2
huì *meeting* 5
huǒchē *train* 5

jǐ *how many?* (usually less than ten) 4
jǐ *crowded* 7
jǐ hào? *which number?* 3
jiā *home* 9
jià(qī) *holiday, vacation* 8
jiàn *(measure word for clothes)* 7
jiào *to call; to be called* 2
jiè (yān) *to give up (smoking)* 10
jié hūn *to marry* 4

Chinese–English vocabulary 169

jié zhàng   to pay the bill   10
jiějie   elder sister   4
jiěmèi   sisters   4
-jíle   (suffix) extremely   10
jīn   half a kilogram   7
jìn   to enter   1
jìn   near   7
jīngjù   Peking opera   6
jīnnián   this year   4
jīntiān   today   1
jiù   just, only   7
juéde   to feel; to think   8
júzizhī   orange juice   10

kāi (huì)   to have (a meeting)   5
kāi (mén)   to open (a door)   5
kāishǐ   to start; start   5
kàn   to look at, to watch   5
kàn(yi)kàn   to have a look   5
kěkǒukělè   cola   10
kěshì   but   4
kěxī   it's a pity   5
kuài   (Chinese unit of money)   7
kuài   fast   8

là   hot, spicy   10
lái   to come   1
lái   I'll have (colloquial)   10
lán(sè) (de)   blue   7
lǎoshī   teacher   1
le   (grammatical marker)   4
lèi   tired; tiring   9
lí   distance from   7
liǎng   two (of anything)   4
liàng   (measure word for things with wheels e.g. car, train, bicycle)   5
líng   zero   3
lóu   floor; building   7
lù   road, street   3
lǜ(sè) (de)   green   7

Lúndūn   London   3

ma   (question particle)   1
mǎi   to buy   6
mài   to sell   7
mǎlù   road   9
māma   mum, mother   4
màn   slow   8
màoxiǎn   adventurous; to take a risk   9
máoyī   woollen pullover   7
mápó dòufu   spicy beancurd/tofu   10
méi   no, not, (have not)   2
měi   every   8
méi guānxi   it's OK, it doesn't matter   2
méi shénme   it's nothing, don't mention it   9
méi wèntí   no problem   6
měi tiān   every day   8
Měiguó   USA   3
mèimei   younger sister   4
mén   door   5
míngnián   next year   5
míngpiàn   namecard   3
míngtiān   tomorrow   1
míngtiān jiàn   see you tomorrow   1
míngzi   name   2
mō(mo)   to feel; to touch   8

nǎ/něi   which?   3/7
nà/nèi   that   2
nǎli nǎli   not really (response to a compliment)   8
nàme   in that case, then   6
nán   male   2
nán   difficult   6
nán   south   9
nánkàn   ugly   8

nǎr?/nǎli? *where?* 3
nàr/nàli *there* 9
ne (question particle) 2
nǐ *you* (singular) 1
nián *year* 4
niánqīng *young* 4
nǐde *your* 2
nǐmen *you* (plural) 1
nín *you* (polite form) 2
nǚ'ér *daughter* 4

pà *afraid* 9
pàng *overweight* 10
péngyou *friend* 2
piányi *cheap* 8
piào *ticket* 3
piàoliang *beautiful* 2
píjiǔ *beer* 16
píngguǒ *apple* 7
pútao *grapes* 7
pútáojiǔ *wine* 10

qí *to ride* 9
qiān *thousand* 7
qián *money* 6
qián *front, ahead* 9
qìchē *vehicle, bus* 9
qǐng *to invite; please* 1
qīngcài *vegetables* 10
qīngchu *clear* 8
qiūtiān *autumn* 14
qū *district, area* 3
qù *to go to* 5
qǔxiāo *to cancel* 5

ràng *to let, allow* 10
ránhòu *afterwards* 6
rè *hot* 10
rén *person* 3

rènshi *to recognize, to know* (people) 2
Rìběn *Japan* 3
róngyì *easy* 6
ròu *meat* 10

shàng *on* 5
shàng bān *to go to work* 9
shàng cì *last time* 10
shāngdiàn *shop* 6
shàngwǔ *morning* 5
shǎo *few; less* 10
shéi/shuí? *who?* 2
shēngrì *birthday* 5
shénme? *what?* 2
shénme shíhou? *when?, what time?* 6
shēntǐ *health; body* 10
shì *to be* 2
shìchǎng *market* 7
shìhé *to suit* 7
shìshi *to try* 7
shōu *to accept; to receive* 10
shūfu *comfortable* 9
shuō *to speak, to say* 2
suàn-cuò le *calculated wrongly* 10
Sūgélán *Scotland* 3
...suì ...*years old; age* 4
suíbiàn *casually* 10

tā *he; she; it* 1
tāde *his; her; its* 2
tài...le! *too...!* 7
tàitai *Mrs; wife* 1
tāng *soup* 10
tānzi *stall* 10
tiān *day* 9

Chinese–English vocabulary **171**

tián (de) sweet 7
tiānqi weather 10
tīng to listen to 6
tīng (measure word for cans of drink) 10
tīngshuō I heard, I am told 9
tuìxiū to retire 9

wǎn bowl 10
wǎng/wàng in the direction of 9
wǎnshang evening 5
wèi (measure word for person (polite)) 2
Wēi'ěrshì Wales 3
wèishénme? why? 10
wēixiǎn dangerous 9
wèn to ask 1
wèntí question, problem 6
wǒ I; me 2
wǒde my 2
wǒmen we; us 2

xī west 9
xià chē to get off (a vehicle) 9
xià yǔ to rain 8
xià (yí +measure word) next 5, 9
xiān first 6
xiǎng would like to; to think 6
xiàng to (look) like 4
Xiānggǎng Hong Kong 9
xiāngjiāo banana 7
xiànjīn cash 10
xiànmu to envy 9
xiānsheng Mr; husband; gentleman 1
xiànzài now 5
xiǎo little, small; young 1
xiǎojie Miss; young woman 2
xiàwǔ afternoon 5
xièxie (nǐ) to thank; thank you 1

Xīfāng the West, Western 6
xǐhuan to like 3
xīn new 8
xíng OK 9
xìng surname 2
xīngqī week 5
xīnxian fresh 7
xìnyòngkǎ credit card 10
xiōngdì brothers 4
xiūxi to rest 6
xué(xí) to study, to learn 8

yánsè color 8
yào to want; to need; will 6
yào it takes... 9
yě also 2
yí ge... yí ge one..., the other 4
yí kè a quarter (time) 5
Yìdàlì Italy 8
yìdiǎn(r) a little 2
yídìng certainly, definitely 6
yígòng altogether 10
yǐhòu later, in future; after 8
yǐjīng already 5
Yīngguó Britain (often also used for England) 3
Yīngwén English (language) 2
yínháng bank 6
yīnyuè music 6
yīnyuèhuì concert 6
yīnyuèjù musical 7
yìqǐ together 9
yǐqián before, in the past 8
yìsi meaning 3
yǐwéi to think, to assume 5
yíyàng same 6
yòng to use; to need 9
yònggōng hardworking 5
yǒu to have 2
yǒu yìdiǎn(r) a little 8

yǒu yìsi *interesting* 6
yòu... yòu... *both... and...* 9
yú *fish* 10
yuǎn *far* 7
yùdìng *to book* (a table, a room) 10
yuè *month* 5
Yuènán *Vietnam* 3

zài *to be at/in* 1
zài (indicating continuing action) 6
zàijiàn *goodbye* 1
zájì *acrobatics* 6
zánmen *we/us* (including listener) 7
zǎo jiù *for a long time, for ages; ages ago* 8
zǎoshang *morning* 5
zěnme? *how?* 9
zěnmeyàng? *how is it? how about it?* 8
zhàn *(bus) stop, station* 7
zhāng (measure word for flat objects) 8
zhàntái *platform* 5
zhè/zhèi *this* 2
zhème (gui) *so (expensive)* 7

zhēn *real; really* 2
zhēnde *really* 4
zhèr *here, this place* 7
zhī (measure word for cigarettes) 10
zhǐ *only* 10
zhǐ yào *only need/cost* 8
zhīdào *to know* 5
zhìliàng *quality* 8
Zhōngguó *China* 3
Zhōngguó-rén *Chinese* 3
Zhōngwén *Chinese* (language) 2
zhōngwǔ *noon* 5
zhōumò *weekend* 5
zhù (nǐ) *to wish (you)* 5
zhù (zài) *to live (in/at a place)* 3
zhǔyì *idea* 8
zì *(Chinese) character*
zìxíngchē *bicycle* 9
zìyóu *free; freedom* 7
zǒu (lù) *to walk, to go on foot* 7
zuì *the most* 7
zuò *to sit* 1
zuò *to do* 6
zuò chē *to take the bus* 6
zuò qìgōng *to do qigong* 6
zúqiú *football* 8

Chinese–English vocabulary

English–Chinese vocabulary

Please note that some of the words below have not appeared in the dialogues within the book. The list is provided as a convenient companion for your reference.

afternoon xiàwǔ
afterwards ránhòu
alcohol jiǔ
all + noun suǒyǒude + noun
all, both dōu
already yǐjīng
also yě
always zǒngshì
America Měiguó
apple píngguǒ
arrangement; to arrange ānpái
to ask wèn
assistant, housestaff fúwùyuán
autumn qiūtiān

bag bāo
bank yínháng
banquet yànhuì
bathroom xǐzǎojiān
to be shì
to be at/in zài
beautiful měi, piàoliang
because yīnwei
beer píjiǔ
before yǐqián
bicycle zìxíngchē
big dà
birthday shēngrì
black hēi(sè) (de)
blue lán(sè) (de)
to board (a vehicle) shàng (chē)

boiled water kāishuǐ
book shū
to book (a ticket) dìng (piào)
both dōu
bottle píng(zi)
breakfast zǎocān/zǎofàn
broken, not working; bad huài
bus gōnggòng qìchē
business shēngyi
but kěshì
to buy mǎi

to call; to be called jiào
camera zhàoxiàngjī
can, be able to néng
can, know how to huì
to cancel qǔxiāo
car qìchē
cash xiànjīn
certainly, definitely yídìng
to change huàn
to change money huàn qián
cheap piányi
Cheers! Gān bēi!
child háizi
China Zhōngguó
Chinese (language) Zhōngwén
Chinese characters Hànzì
chocolate qiǎokèlì
to choose xuǎnzé
chopsticks kuàizi

city chéngshì
clean gānjìng
clear qīngchu
clever cōngming
to close (a door) guān (mén)
coach (vehicle) chángtú qìchē
coffee kāfēi
cold lěng
cold, cool liáng(kuai)
colleague tóngshì
to come lái
to come back huí lái
comfortable shūfu
company gōngsī
computer diànnǎo
concert yīnyuèhuì
convenient fāngbiàn
to cook zuò (fàn)
cough; to cough késou
country guójiā
credit card xìnyòngkǎ
crowded jǐ
cup(ful) bēi

dad, father bàba
dangerous wēixiǎn
daughter nǚ'ér
day tiān
to decide juédìng
delicious, tasty hǎochī (de)
difficult nán
dish cài
to do zuò
doctor yīshēng, dàifu
don't bié
door mén
double room shuāngrén fángjiān
downstairs lóuxià
to drink hē
to drive kāi

early zǎo
east dōng
easy róngyì
to eat chī
economy jīngjì
elder brother gēge
elder sister jiějie
e-mail diànzǐ yóujiàn/ yīmèi'ér
embassy dàshǐguǎn
English (language) Yīngwén
to enter jìn
euro ōuyuán
every měi
everyone dàjiā
everything yíqiè
excuse me duìbuqǐ
expensive; honourable guì
extremely fēicháng, -jíle

far yuǎn
fast kuài
fault cuò
to feel; to think juéde
few; less shǎo
to fill in (a form) tián (biǎo)
film, movie diànyǐng
first xiān
fish yú
floor, story lóu
food, meal fàn
football zúqiú
for; to give gěi
foreign country wàiguó
foreign enterprise wàizī qǐyè
form biǎo
free; freedom zìyóu
friend péngyou
friendly yǒuhǎo
friendship yǒuyì

English–Chinese vocabulary

from cóng
fruit shuǐguǒ

to get off the bus xià chē
to go back huí qù
to go to qù, dào
good; well hǎo
goodbye zàijiàn
green lǜ(sè) (de)
guest kèren

half bàn
hand shǒu
happy gāoxìng/kuàilè
hard working yònggōng
to have yǒu
to have a cold gǎnmào
to have diarrhoea lā dùzi
he; she; it tā
headache tóu téng
health; body shēntǐ
health; healthy jiànkāng
to help bāng
here, this place zhèr
to hire, to rent zū
his; her; its tāde
holiday, vacation jià(qī)
home jiā
to hope; hope xīwàng
hospital yīyuàn
hot rè
hot, spicy là
hotel fàndiàn, bīnguǎn, lǚguǎn
hour xiǎoshí
how? zěnme?
how far? duō yuǎn?
how is it? how about it? zěnmeyàng?
how much? how many? duōshao?
hundred bǎi

hungry è
husband xiānsheng, àiren

I; me wǒ
idea zhǔyì
identity card shēnfènzhèng
if rúguǒ, yàoshi
illness bìng
to inform tōngzhī
inside lǐ
interest xìngqu
interesting yǒu yìsi
international guójì
interpreter, translator; to interpret, translate fānyì
to introduce; introduction jièshào
to invite; please qǐng

joint venture hézī qǐyè

key yàoshi
kilogram gōngjīn
knife and fork dāochā
to know (a fact) zhīdao
to know (people) rènshi

language yǔyán
last zuìhòu
later, after yǐhòu
to leave; to walk zǒu
left zuǒ
to let, to allow ràng
letter xìn
letter box xìnxiāng
light dēng
to look like xiàng
to like xǐhuan
to listen to tīng
a little yìdiǎn(r)
little, small; young xiǎo

to live (in/at a place) zhù (zài)
long cháng
to look at, to watch kàn
to look for zhǎo
to lose diū
to love; love ài

male nán
many; more duō
to marry jié hūn
meaning yìsi
meat ròu
medicine yào
to meet jiàn miàn
meeting huì
menu càidān
minute fēn(zhōng)
Miss; young woman xiǎojie
to miss (a person) xiǎng
mobile (phone) shǒujī
money qián
month yuè
morning shàngwǔ
morning (early) zǎoshang
most zuì
mountain shān
mountain bike shāndìchē
Mr; husband; gentleman xiānsheng
Mrs; wife tàitai
mum, mother māma
music yīnyuè
musical yīnyuèjù

near jìn
to need; must; it takes děi
new xīn
news; information xiāoxi
next xià (yí +measure word)
nice looking hǎokàn
no, not, (have not) méi

noisy chǎo
north běi
not bù
not bad, pretty good búcuò
now xiànzài
number hào
number (phone) hàomǎ
nurse hùshi

o'clock diǎn(zhōng)
of course dāngrán
often chángcháng
old lǎo
Olympic Games Àolínpǐkè Yùndònghuì
on shàng
only zhǐ
opportunity jīhuì
opposite duìmiàn
other biéde
overweight pàng

pain; painful téng
park gōngyuán
passport hùzhào
to pay (money) fù qián
peace hépíng
person rén
pharmacy yàofáng
phone diànhuà
place dìfang
to plan dǎsuàn
plane fēijī
platform zhàntái
pleasant; happy yúkuài
police officer jǐngchá
polite kèqi
possible; possibly kěnéng
to post jì
post office yóujú

English–Chinese vocabulary 177

postcard míngxìnpiàn
pound (money) (Yīng)bàng
to phone dǎ diànhuà
to practise; to exercise liànxí
prescription yàofāng
pretty good búcuò
purse, wallet qiánbāo
to put fàng

question; problem wèntí
quiet ānjìng

rain yǔ
to rain xià yǔ
real; really zhēn
really zhēnde
reason yuányīn
receipt shōujù
recent; recently zuìjìn
to recognize; to know (people) rènshi
red hóng(sè) (de)
to rest xiūxi
to return something (to) huán (gěi)
right (the opposite of left) yòu
road, street lù
room fángjiān

safe ānquán
same yíyàng
sandwich sānmíngzhì
satisfied mǎnyì
seat wèizi
to see kàn-jiàn
to see a doctor kàn bìng, kàn yīshēng
to seem hǎoxiàng
to sell mài
service fúwù
ship, boat chuán

a short while; after a moment yìhuǐ(r)
sightseeing yóulǎn
simple jiǎndān
to sing (a song) chàng (gē)
single room dānrén fángjiān
to sit zuò
size dàxiǎo
to sleep shuì
slim shòu
slow màn
to smoke (a cigarette) chōu (yān)
to snow xià xuě
so, therefore suǒyǐ
some yìxiē, yǒude
sometimes yǒu shíhou
son érzi
soup tāng
south nán
to speak, to say shuō
sports; to take exercise yùndòng
spring chūntiān
stamp yóupiào
to start kāishǐ
station, (bus) stop (chē) zhàn
still hái
to stroll sàn bù
student xuésheng
to study, to learn xué(xí)
success; successful chénggōng
sugar táng
summer xiàtiān
sunny (day) qíngtiān
surname xìng
sweet tián (de)
to swim yóuyǒng

to take a holiday dù jià
to take the bus zuò chē
to take, to fetch ná

to talk, chat tán
taxi chūzū (qì)chē
tea chá
teacher lǎoshī
television diànshì
to tell gàosu
to thank; thank you xièxie (nǐ)
that nà/nèi
there nàr/nàli
these; those zhèixiē/nèixiē
they; them tāmen
thing, matter, issue shìqing
thing, object dōngxi
to think, to believe rènwéi
to think, to assume yǐwéi
this zhè/zhèi
this year jīnnián
thousand qiān
ticket piào
time shíjiān
time, occasion cì
tired; tiring lèi
to arrive; to go to dào
today jīntiān
together yìqǐ
toilet cèsuǒ
tomorrow míngtiān
too . . . ! tài . . . le!
train huǒchē
transport, traffic jiāotōng
to travel; travel lǚxíng, lǚyóu
to try shìshi
to turn guǎi
TV diànshì
two (of anything) liǎng

underground, subway dìtiě
to understand dǒng, míngbai
university dàxué
upstairs lóushàng

to use yòng
US dollar měiyuán
usually yìbān

vegetables qīngcài
vehicle (bus, bike, car) chē
very hěn
video (tape) lùxiàngdài
visa qiānzhèng
visit; to visit (formal) fǎngwèn

to wait děng
to walk, to go on foot zǒu lù
to want (to); to need; will yào
to want to, would like to xiǎng
warm nuǎn(huo)
water shuǐ
we, us wǒmen
weather tiānqi
week xīngqī
weekend zhōumò
to welcome; welcome huānyíng
west xī
what? shénme?
what kind? shénme yàng de?
when, what time? shénme shíhou?
where? nǎr?/nǎli?
which? nǎ/něi?
which number? jǐ hào?
white bái(sè) (de)
who? shéi?/shuí?
whose? shéide?/shuíde?
why? wèishénme?
wife tàitai, àiren
wife (formal); *madam* fūren
wind fēng
wine pútáojiǔ
winter dōngtiān
to work; work gōngzuò
to write xiě

English–Chinese vocabulary

year nián
... *year* (of age) ... suì
yellow huáng(sè) (de)
yes; correct duì
you (singular) nǐ
you (polite form) nín

you (plural) nǐmen
young niánqīng
younger brother dìdi
younger sister mèimei
your (singular) nǐde
your (plural) nǐmende

Appendix: character texts

UNIT 1 HELLO! HOW ARE YOU?
第一课 你好！你好吗？

Dialogue 1

格林太太	你好，小王！
格林先生	小王，你好!
小王	格林先生，格林太太，你们好！
格林太太	你太太好吗？
小王	她很好，谢谢。

Dialogue 2

格林先生	小王，谢谢你。
格林太太	谢谢你，小王。
小王	不用谢。
格林先生	再见。
小王	再见。
格林太太	再见。

Dialogue 3

李先生	请进。
格林先生	(enters the room)
李先生	格林先生，你好！
格林先生	你好，李先生。
李先生	请坐。
格林先生	谢谢。

李先生	格林太太好吗？
格林先生	她很好。谢谢。

Dialogue 4

Frank	请问，张老师在吗？
李老师	对不起，她不在。
Frank	她今天来吗？
李老师	不来。她明天来。
Frank	谢谢你。
李老师	不用谢。明天见。
Frank	明天见。

UNIT 2 WHAT'S YOUR NAME?
第二课 你叫什么？

Dialogue 1

Jane	您贵姓？
陈	我姓陈。您呢？
Jane	我姓 Lord。这是您的孩子吗？
陈	不是。我没有孩子。这是李太太的孩子。
Jane	(to the boy) 你叫什么名字？
孩子	我叫盼盼。

Dialogue 2

White	郑先生，你好！
常	我姓常，不姓郑。我叫常正。
White	对不起，常先生。
常	没关系。White 先生，你有没有中文名字？

White	有。我叫白彼德。
常	白先生，你会不会说英文？
White	当然会。常先生，你也会说英文吗？
常	会一点儿。

Dialogue 3

白	那是谁？你认识不认识她？
吴	认识。她是郭小姐。
白	她真漂亮。
	……
白	你好！我叫白比德。你呢？
郭	你好，我叫郭玉婕。
	……
郭	这是我的男朋友。他叫刘文光。这是白先生。
刘	白先生，你好！
白	哦，你好！

UNIT 3 WHERE ARE YOU FROM?
第三课 你是哪国人？

Dialogue 1

林	您是哪国人？
白	我是英国人。这是我的名片。
林	谢谢。哦，白先生，你住在伦敦？
白	对。你是中国人吧？
林	是，我是广东人。

Dialogue 2

Officer	请给我看看您的飞机票。
白	这是我的飞机票。
Officer	你住在什么饭店?
白	和平饭店。
Officer	和平饭店?
白	对,和平是peace的意思。我喜欢和平。
Officer	谢谢您。

Dialogue 3

林	你住在哪儿?
白	我住在和平饭店。
林	几号房间?
白	五零八号房间。你住在哪儿?
林	我住在平安路七号。
白	平安路在哪儿?
林	平安路在西城区。
白	和平饭店也在西城区,是不是?
林	不在。在东城区。
白	你的电话号码是多少?
林	六五五二 九三二四。你的呢?
白	我的是六六七三 八八三零。

UNIT 4 DO YOU HAVE BROTHERS AND SISTERS?
第四课 你有兄弟、姐妹吗?

Dialogue 1

| 丁 | 您叫什么名字? |
| 刘 | 我叫刘富贵。 |

丁	刘先生结婚了吗？
刘	结婚了。
丁	有没有孩子？
刘	有两个，一个儿子，一个女儿。
丁	他们几岁？
刘	儿子两岁，女儿五岁。

Dialogue 2

丁	您有兄弟、姐妹吗？
刘	有两个弟弟、一个妹妹。没有哥哥和姐姐。
丁	您弟弟、妹妹多大？
刘	大弟弟二十六，小弟弟二十四。
丁	妹妹呢？
刘	妹妹二十八。
丁	很好，谢谢您。
刘	不客气。
丁	再见！
刘	再见！

Dialogue 3

吴	你爸爸、妈妈多大年纪？
陆	爸爸五十三，妈妈四十九。
吴	不像，不像。这是你妹妹吧。她真年轻。
陆	她今年二十二。
吴	真的？她结婚了吗？
陆	没有。可是有男朋友了。
吴	哦。

Appendix: character texts

UNIT 5 WHAT TIME IS IT NOW?
第五课 几点了？

Dialogue 1

营业员	喂，和平超市，您好。
顾客*	请问，你们几点开门？
营业员	上午八点到下午五点半。
顾客	中午关门吗？
营业员	不关。
顾客	周末开不开？
营业员:	星期六和星期天都开。
*顾客	gùkè *customer*

Dialogue 2

小许	现在几点了？
老万	两点一刻了。
小许	噢，会已经开始了。
老万	什么会？你不是明天开会吗？
小许	今天星期几？
老万	星期三。
小许	噢，我还以为是星期四呢。

Dialogue 3

Selena	您去哪儿？
马特	我去利物浦。
Selena	几点的火车？哪个站台？
马特	我不知道。我的火车取消了。

Selena	我帮您看看。(Looks at the notice board)
	啊,下一辆是三点一刻,在第六站台。
马特	现在三点差五分,还有二十分钟。
Selena	祝您一路顺风。
马特	谢谢您。再见。

Dialogue 4

Ann	明年春节是几月几号?
朋友	二月十二号。
Ann	真可惜。我的生日是二月十一号。
朋友	没关系。英国十一号的晚上就是中国十二号的早上。

UNIT 6 WHAT DO YOU WANT TO DO TODAY?
第六课 你今天想做什么?

Dialogue 1

小吴	今天休息。你想做什么?
Frank	我想去买东西。可是我要先换钱。
小吴	好。我们先坐车去银行换钱,然后去商店买东西。
Frank	好。下午我想去北海公园。
小吴	没问题。晚上呢?
Frank	晚上我们去看杂技好不好?
小吴	太好了。我请服务员给我们订票。

Appendix: character texts

Dialogue 2

小吴	今天晚上你想看电影还是看京剧?
Frank	我不喜欢京剧。
小吴	那么我们看电影吧。电影比京剧有意思。
Frank	有没有音乐会?
小吴	你想听中国音乐还是听西方音乐?
Frank	在中国当然听中国音乐。

Dialogue 3

Frank	早上好!
Passer-by	早上好!
Frank	他在做什么?
Passer-by	他在打太极拳。
Frank	那个人也在打太极拳吗?
Passer-by	不。他在做气功。
Frank	气功跟太极拳一样吗?
Passer-by	不一样。
Frank	气功比太极拳难吗?
Passer-by	不一定。我说气功比太极拳容易。

UNIT 7 HOW MUCH IS IT?
第七课 多少钱?

Dialogue 1

| 顾客 | 请问,在哪儿买毛衣? |
| 营业员 | 在二楼。 |

………

| 营业员 | 您买什么? |

顾客	我想买一件毛衣。
营业员	要哪件？您喜欢什么颜色的？
顾客	那件红色的给我看看行吗？
营业员	这件很好。
顾客	哦，太大了。那件黄色的我试试可以吗？
营业员	这件也不错。
顾客	哦，太小了。
营业员	这件蓝色的很适合你。
顾客	太好了。多少钱？
营业员	五百块。
顾客	嗯，太贵了。对不起，谢谢你。
营业员	……

Dialogue 2

小芳	我们去自由市场看看吧。
Ann	好。自由市场离这儿多远？
小芳	很近。坐车两、三站就到了。
Ann	车太挤了。咱们走路去吧。
小芳	可是走路太远了。
Ann	走路要多长时间？
小芳	走路要二、三十分钟才能到。
Ann	好吧。那么咱们坐车去吧。

Dialogue 3

顾客	苹果怎么卖？
摊贩	四块一斤。
顾客	真贵！他们的苹果三块八一斤。
摊贩	可是我的苹果比他们的大一点儿。

顾客	葡萄多少钱一斤？
摊贩	四块两毛五一斤。
顾客	这么贵！他们的四块一斤。
摊贩	可是我的葡萄比他们的甜多了。
顾客	草莓一斤多少钱？
摊贩	八块二。
顾客	太贵了！
摊贩	可是我的草莓比他们的新鲜得多！
顾客	你的东西最贵。
摊贩	可是我的东西最好！

UNIT 8 WHAT'S IT LIKE?
第八课 怎么样？

Dialogue 1

素兰	这是我新买的毛衣。你看怎么样？
Eli	不错，不错。
素兰	大小合适吗？
Eli	嗯，有点儿大。
素兰	颜色好看吗？
Eli	嗯，不难看。
素兰	你摸模……你觉得质量怎么样？
Eli	嗯，还可以。多少钱？
素兰	不贵，只要一百五十块。
Eli	什么？！一百五十块我可以买三张足球票！

Dialogue 2

| 罗太太 | 假期过得好吗？ |
| 李先生 | 非常好，就是东西不便宜。 |

罗太太	我早就知道了。
李先生	我以前觉得英国的东西贵,现在才知道法国的东西更贵。
罗太太	意大利的东西也很贵是不是?
李先生	意大利的东西也不比法国的便宜。你的假期过得怎么样?
罗太太	不怎么样。
李先生	怎么了?
罗太太	每天都下雨。

Dialogue 3

宝婕	你的中文说得真好。
Martin	哪里,哪里。我的中文没有你的英文好。
宝婕	不。你的中文比我的英文好得多。
Martin	以后我帮你学英文,你帮我学中文,怎么样?
宝婕	好主意。可是我学得不快。
Martin	没关系,我学得也很慢。

UNIT 9 HOW DO I GET TO . . . ?
第九课 去......怎么走?

Dialogue 1

乔	听说你快要去度假了。
冯	对,我有三个星期的假,从六月二十七号到七月十八号。
乔	你打算去哪儿?
冯	香港和澳门。这两个地方我都没去过。

乔	你怎么去？
冯	我先坐飞机到香港，在那儿住五天。再从香港坐船到澳门。
乔	我真羡慕你。
冯	你什么时候度假？
乔	我？噢，十二月。
冯	多长时间？
乔	不知道。
冯	怎么会不知道？
乔	今年十二月我就要退休了。
冯	我真羡慕你。

Dialogue 2

Paola	请问，去天坛怎么走？
Passer-by	天坛在西南边儿。坐车四站就到了。
Paola	坐几路车？
Passer-by	你先从这儿往东走。再坐往南开的车，十五路、二十三路都行。车站在银行对面儿。
Paola	用换车吗？
Passer-by	不用。下车以后往前走一点儿。天坛就在马路西边儿。
Paola	谢谢您。
Passer-by	没什么。

Dialogue 3

James	你去过天津吗？
黄	没去过。
James	下个周末咱们一起去吧。

黄	好啊。你打算怎么去？坐汽车还是坐火车？
James	咱们骑车去，怎么样？
黄	什么？你发疯了！骑车去天津要两、三天，又累又危险。
James	我不怕累，也喜欢冒险！
黄	反正我不跟你一起去。我在家看电视，又舒服又安全。

UNIT 10 WHAT WOULD YOU LIKE TO EAT?
第十课 您想吃什么？

Dialogue 1

服务员	你们预订了吗？
Mr Hussein	预订了。我叫 Omar Hussein.
服务员	我看一看。……Mr Hussein, 七点半，两个人。
Mr Hussein	对，对。
服务员	好，请跟我来。
	……
服务员	这是菜单。你们先喝点儿什么？
余乔	我要一杯桔子汁。
Mr Hussein	你们有什么葡萄酒？
服务员	我们有长城白葡萄酒和中国红葡萄酒。
Mr Hussein	来一杯白葡萄酒吧。
	……
服务员	酒来了。你们要什么菜？
余乔	我不吃肉。

Appendix: character texts   193

Mr Hussein	你吃不吃鱼？
余乔	不吃。我只要青菜和豆腐。
Mr Hussein	什么？你现在吃素了？
余乔	是啊。我已经很胖了。
服务员	你们喜欢吃辣的吗？
余乔	喜欢。可是别太辣了。
服务员	来一个麻婆豆腐吧。
Mr Hussein	好啊。先来两个酸辣汤。
余乔	今天已经很热了，我们应该少吃辣的。
服务员	没关系。吃完饭以后，你们多吃点儿冰淇淋。我们的冰淇淋非常好吃。

Dialogue 2

Mr Hussein	喝杯咖啡吧。
余乔	不喝了。
Mr Hussein	为什么？我知道你爱喝咖啡。
余乔	太晚了，我怕影响睡觉。
Mr Hussein	我不怕。那你喝杯(珍珠奶)茶 *吧？
余乔	那来一杯吧。… 真好喝！
Mr Hussein	… 你吃饱了吗？
余乔	吃饱了。
Mr Hussein	我们结账吧。服务员，买单。
服务员	你们吃好了吗？
余乔	吃好了，谢谢。
Mr Hussein	你们收不收信用卡？
服务员	对不起，我们只收现金。

*珍珠奶茶 bubble tea

Dialogue 3

Ann	我饿了,我们随便吃点儿吧。
方	那儿有个小摊子,他们的炒面好吃极了。
	……
方	请来两碗儿炒面、两听可口可乐。
服务员	请先付钱。两碗儿炒面五十块,两听可口可乐十块,一共六十块。
方	什么?你算错了吧。上次炒面二十块一碗儿。
服务员	没算错。上次是上次,现在一碗儿二十五块了。

Taking it further

If you would like to extend your ability so that you can develop your confidence, fluency and scope in the language, whether for social or business purposes, why not take your Chinese a step further with *Complete Mandarin Chinese*?

You could see if there are any Mandarin Chinese language classes taking place in your area. Many big universities have Chinese departments or language centres which run courses in a number of foreign languages including Mandarin Chinese. Large cities often have an annual publication listing all the courses taking place that year and where they are held.

You can also go online and look at the following websites, but do remember these are constantly changing and new ones are being added all the time.

Pinyin practice: http://www.ctcfl.ox.ac.uk/Pinyin_Notes.htm – Everything you need to know about pinyin.

https://yoyochinese.com/chinese-learning-tools/Mandarin-Chinese-pronunciation-lesson/pinyin-chart-table – pinyin with the indication of tones.

For beginners: http://www.bbc.co.uk/languages/chinese/ and http://www.bbc.co.uk/languages/chinese/real_chinese/ – a good starting point.

More comprehensive websites: https://www.purpleculture.net/ – Check out the 'Chinese tools' section.

https://resources.allsetlearning.com/chinese/grammar/ – for grammar at all levels. It also contains a simple but helpful 'Learner FAQ'.

http://www.mandarintools.com/ – another site which has many links to China-related websites.

All the instructions are in English. English and Chinese (simplified characters). Online English–Chinese and Chinese–English dictionary. Illustration of stroke order.

IMAGE CREDITS

1. Monkey Business Images / Shutterstock.com
3. aslysun / Shutterstock.com
4. Monkey Business Images / Shutterstock.com
5. Matthew Benoit / Shutterstock.com
6. Jack.Q / Shutterstock.com
7. fsghhc / Shutterstock.com
8. Mitrofanova / Shutterstock.com
9. Professional Photography / Shutterstock.com
10. eugena-klykova / Shutterstock.com

Can-do statements

UNIT	CEFR level	ACTFL level	CAN-DO STATEMENTS
UNIT 1	A1	Novice High	I can establish basic social contact by using simple everyday forms of greetings, farewells and introductions.
UNIT 2	A1	Novice High	I can go one step beyond establishing basic social contact by requesting and receiving personal information.
UNIT 3	A1	Novice High	I can give basic personal information, understand and use numbers and have mastered some relevant nationalities and countries.
UNIT 4	A1	Novice High	I can give personal information, especially about one's family, understand and use numbers.
UNIT 5	A2	Intermediate Low	I can tell the time. I can express days of the week and dates.
UNIT 6	A1 / A2	Novice High / Intermediate Low	I can make requests and suggestions, talk about leisure activities, use the comparative and use the correct word order for adverbial phrases of time, manner and place.

UNIT	CEFR level	ACTFL level	CAN-DO STATEMENTS
UNIT 7	A1 / A2	Novice High / Intermediate Low	I can understand and use bigger numbers. I can understand and use prices when going shopping, make more complex comparisons, use connecting words and superlatives.
UNIT 8	A1 / A2	Novice High / Intermediate Low	I can make requests and suggestions, talk about leisure activities, use the comparative and use the correct word order for adverbial phrases of time, manner and place.
UNIT 9	A1 / A2	Novice High / Intermediate Low	I can understand questions and instructions addressed carefully and slowly. I can follow short, simple directions.
UNIT 10	A2	Intermediate Low	(Food and drink) I can use past simple, can use linkers: sequential-past time; more on measure words; commands.